THE NEXT GENERATION

Understanding and Meeting the Needs of Generation X

GARY ZUSTIAK

COLLEGE PRESS PUBLISHING COMPANY • JOPLIN, MISSOURI

Copyright 1996
College Press Publishing Co.

Cover design: Daryl Williams

Library of Congress Cataloging-in-Publication Data

Zustiak, Gary Blair, 1952–
    The next generation: understanding and meeting the needs
of generation X / Gary B. Zustiak.
        p.   cm.
    Includes bibliographical references and index.
    ISBN 0-89900-763-5 (pbk.)
    1. Church work with young adults.   2. Generation X—
Religious life.   3. Generation X—Psychology.   4. Evangelistic
work.   I. Title.
BV4446.Z87 1996
253—dc20   96-21348
                                                  CIP

DEDICATION

The writing of this book has brought me to an even greater
appreciation for the family I was privileged to grow up in.
As I have listened to hundreds of young people tell me their stories
about neglect and abuse in their homes, I realize how fortunate
I was to have two loving parents who raised me in a supportive
Christian home. If I haven't said it before — "Thanks mom and dad."
When I think of Generation X, I think of my three favorite
Xers, Joshua, Aaron and Caleb. I want you to know
that you have always been a source of joy and pride for
me. The years went by too quickly. I hope that
I was able to teach you half of what you taught me
about the important things in life.
This book is also for Alicia, my beautiful granddaughter.
She is part of the Millennial Generation. I pray that
her future is bright and filled with hope, unlike
the generation that preceded her.
More than anyone I have Mary, the wife of my youth, to
thank for her unending support, encouragement and
participation through more than twenty years
of youth ministry. Thanks for always being there
and having the patience to raise "four" boys.
I love you.

ACKNOWLEDGMENTS

I want to acknowledge a number of people who have contributed to the support and writing of this book. First of all, I want to thank John Hunter, my editor, and Chris DeWelt, President of College Press, for giving me the opportunity to present the burden that I have for Generation X to the church at large. I appreciate your confidence in me and your support through this project.

I would be remiss if I did not thank several colleagues, Mark Moore and Mark Scott, for their contributions to this book. Both of them allowed me to "steal" some of their best insights concerning issues pertaining to Generation X. Thanks for being generous with your discoveries and material. I owe you. I know that the Lord will continue to bless your ministries.

The seeds for this book came about as I shared in several workshops my observations and discoveries concerning Generation X at several summer Christ In Youth conferences and the National Youth Leader's Convention. A heartfelt thanks to all the "buds" over at CIY for providing me a forum in which to develop my presentation.

It has been a pleasure to have had the opportunity to teach at Ozark Christian College these past ten years. How I have been ministered to by the mutual encouragement and fellowship that I have received from the faculty, staff and students! You are all the greatest. Thanks for your prayer support and words of encouragement through the writing of this book.

Last, but certainly not least, I want to acknowledge the courage and trust of those members of Generation X who have shared their stories with me and have allowed me to pass them on to you. It is my prayer that your transparency will be the catalyst for others of your generation to tell their story, so that the world might hear about your needs and your hurts — but also about the great love that you have for one another and the desire to serve that you bring from the bottom of your heart. May the grace and peace of the Lord Jesus Christ be yours in abundance.

To the only wise God be glory forever through Jesus Christ!
Amen.
Dr. Gary B. Zustiak

91513

Table of Contents

Introduction 13

Chapter One: Who Is Generation X? 19
   Generation X and Their Place In History 19
   Labels, Labels, Labels 21
   What's In A Name, Anyway? 24
   Life Application and Implication For Ministry 26

Chapter Two: Unwanted: Dead or Alive 29
   The Birth Control Factor 29
   Abortion 31
   Zero Population Growth 31
   Latchkey Kids 32
   Working Mothers 33
   Housing Laws 35
   Movies, Restaurants and the Swinging Single 36
   Life Application and Implication For Ministry 38

Chapter Three: Dysfunction Junction 41
   Divorce and Dysfunction 42
   The Effects of Divorce 44
   Blended Families 46
   Single-Parent Families 48
   Intact Families 49
   Physical and Sexual Abuse 51
   Drug and Alcohol Addictions 52
   Life Application and Implication For Ministry 54

Chapter Four: Why Can't Gen X Read? 59
   The Why Behind the Fall 63
   Incompetent Teachers 65
   How It All Played Out For Generation X 66
   Life Application and Implication For Ministry 69

Chapter Five: Just Do It!
      The Values and Beliefs of Generation X 71
   Exit Absolute Truth 73
   Smorgasbord Spirituality 75

The Politics of Generation X 79
The Sex Generation 82
Concerns of Gen X Teens 86
Generation X and the Work Place 88
Life Application and Implication For Ministry 91

Chapter Six: Overview and Summary .95
School House Woes 96
Soaring Crime 96
Stress, Suicide and Mental Health 97
Sexual Attitudes and Consequences 98
Teenage Runaways and Throwaways 100
Trauma and Survivor's Guilt 100
Hostility 102
Darkness On The Horizon 103
Are There Any Exceptions? 103
Differences Between Boomers and Generation X 107
Life Application and Implication For Ministry 107

Chapter Seven: Worldview 113
The Theistic Worldview 115
The Modern Worldview 121
Summary 126
A Comparison Between the Worldviews
    of Theism and Modernism 129
Life Application and Implication For Ministry 129

Chapter Eight: The Development of a
    Postmodern Worldview 131
The Star Trek Analogy 134
Deconstruction 136
Everything Is Relative 140
What Are the Implications For the Church? 143
Life Application and Implication For Ministry 146

Chapter Nine: Comparing Two Worlds 151
A Loss of Center 152
Biblical Illiteracy 156
Family Fragmentation 157
Secularization of the People of God 157

Legalism On Horizon to Protect Perimeters 158
Religion of Form — Little Substance 160
Neglect of Personal Holiness and Piety 160
Stress Level High Over Lack of Control
      Over One's Destiny 161
Conclusion 162
Life Application and Implication For Ministry 162

Chapter Ten: Gateways to the Soul of Generation X 165
The Need For Community 167
Spirituality 171
Sexuality 174
Mystery 176
Relationships Versus Race and Possessions 177
Family 181
Identity 184
Involvement In Causes 185
Conclusion 187
Life Application and Implication For Ministry 187

Chapter Eleven: Programming to Meet
      the Needs of Generation X 191
Creating a User-Friendly Environment 192
Narrative Evangelism — The Powerful Use of Story 197
Process Evangelism 202
The Need For a New Apologetic 205
Ministry Through Small Groups .206
Reclaiming a Christian Worldview 210
The Content of Our Programs 214
Teaching Generation X 217
Conclusion 220
Life Implication and Application For Ministry 220

Outline 225

Bibliography 231

Index 241

INTRODUCTION

Tim[1] was eleven when it happened. He had no warning, no hints that this might take place. As far as he could tell, he was growing up in a normal, happy all-American family. He was watching TV when his mother came in through the front door that Saturday and announced to the family that she was leaving. She was in love with another man and had come home only to pack her stuff and go.

While his father begged and pleaded with his mother to stay, Tim went out into the field behind the house to pick some wild flowers. When you're only eleven years old, it's tough to know what to do. He was in shock over what was taking place. It all happened so quickly. But Tim thought that picking some wild flowers for his mom would be a good way to tell her that he loved her and was going to miss her.

He gave his mother those hand-picked flowers and told her that he loved her. He didn't want her to go. Tears trickled down the young boy's face. But she was resolute. With suitcase in hand she walked out the front door and headed for the street. She didn't even wait until she was out of sight, but threw that bouquet of flowers into the trash can at the edge of the walk as Tim and his father watched her leave. She got into her car and drove off without looking back, leaving a stunned husband and a brokenhearted little boy standing on the steps weeping. His mother, the one who was supposed to love him, take care of him and protect him was leaving. Gone, never to return. And along with the flowers, she tossed Tim's longings for a normal, happy childhood into the garbage can.

It affected Tim for a long time. He began to build walls of protection around himself. He wasn't ever going to let someone get close to him and hurt him like that ever again. As he grew into adulthood, his relationships with women were always guarded or exploitive. No woman was ever going to hurt him again.

I wish that I could tell you that this was an isolated instance, an anomaly. But for Generation X this is the rule rather than the exception. Generation X saw their families break up in unprecedented numbers. Previously in America (from the years 1950-1960) the divorce rate averaged about 375,000 divorces per year. This involved about a half-million children. But by 1970 the numbers had jumped to 650,000 divorces. Just five years later one million couples split up, affecting 1.1 million children. At least 40% of Generation X are children of divorce. Compare that to only 11% of those born in the fifties.[2]

Unfortunately, divorce is not their only problem. Generation X seems to be the most unwanted, uncared for, maligned, abused and rejected generation to come down the pike. Parents didn't want them, teachers failed them and authority figures betrayed them. So they have rejected the values and morals of those generations who have gone before them. They place a premium upon their relationships with their peer group, hoping to find in their friends the love and acceptance they were denied by family. Like the words in the song by Michael W. Smith, they are searching for "my place in this world."[3]

Is there a place for Generation X? If so, what is it? Do they have a future? Hopefully it is more than just some dead-end McJob.[4] There is a whole generation of broken and hurting kids out there who need healing and hope. I know that healing and wholeness can take place. Remember Tim? Someone invited him to attend one of the praise and reach out gatherings held at Calvary Chapel in California. Through a loving and supportive community Tim became open to the gospel message. Eventually he accepted Jesus Christ as his personal Savior and was baptized. In a singles Bible study he met a beautiful woman who would later become his wife.

Because of the help that he had personally received and the great need that he saw all around him, Tim decided to go into full-time Christian service. He enrolled in Bible college to prepare for the youth ministry. While in school his mother, the same one who had walked out on him when he was a boy, went through a personal crisis. The man she had left her family for walked out on her. She was devastated by this rejection and even became suicidal. Tim and his wife made a special trip to go and be with her and to try and support her through this crisis. They invested a great amount of time and prayer in bringing stability and hope once more into Tim's mother's life. Today she is a Christian and doing fine.

I am still amazed and humbled by Tim's story. How could he find it within himself to forgive his mother for the pain that she had caused him and go out of his way to comfort her in her time of crisis? The natural or carnal response would be to say, "Good! Now you know how I felt. I hope it hurts as bad and for as long as it hurt me." But that wasn't Tim's response. His was one of forgiveness and compassion. It can only be explained through the life-changing power of the gospel of Jesus Christ. Tim will tell you it is so.

It is my belief that the gospel of Jesus Christ is the answer for those of Tim's generation — Generation X. But if they are to hear it, there must be some changes take place in our attitude and understanding towards them. Parents, ministers and youth workers need to understand the world of Generation X — their personal world with all of its pain and frustration, rejection and anger. We need to understand that much of what they got was not of their asking nor desire. They didn't just wake up one morning as a collective group and say, "Hey, let's all be slackers." There were some specific events which took place historically and philosophically which paved the way for the road leading to the development of the personification of Generation X. This is not to say that they don't have a choice or are not responsible for their actions. It simply means that their choices and actions are more understandable when viewed in light of their historical and philosophical situation.

I would like to take you on a journey — a journey through Generation X. On this journey you will learn about the characteristics which shape and make up the life of the typical Xer. You will also learn about the historical events and the philosophical background which assisted in laying the foundation for the development of this next generation. Our journey will end with a look at what will be effective in helping to reach out to the next generation and to give them hope and a future.

Notes

1. Not his real name, but the story is used with his permission.

2. Geoffrey T. Holtz, Welcome to the Jungle: The Why Behind "Generation X." New York: St. Martin's Griffin (1995), 26–27.

3. Michael W. Smith, "My Place In This World," Go West Young Man, Reunion (1990).

4. This expression has gained currency in discussions of the problems of this generation, to represent a low-paying job with little chance for advancement, such as jobs in the fast-food industry. For example, see Holtz, Welcome to the Jungle, 146; and Neil Howe and Bill Strauss, 13th Gen: Abort, Retry, Ignore, Fail? (New York: Vintage Books, 1993), 13.

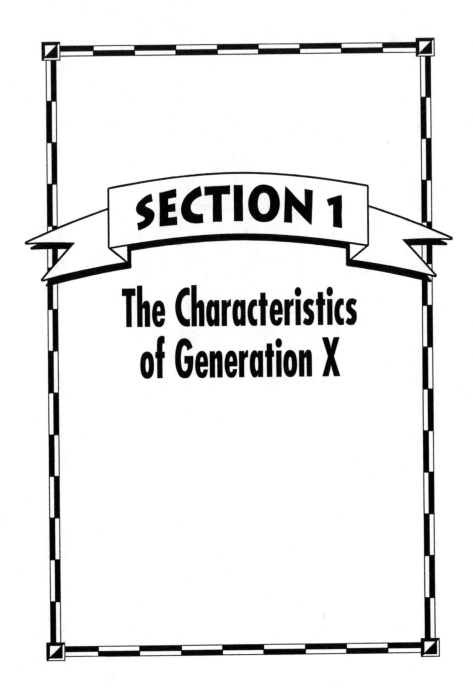

SECTION 1

The Characteristics of Generation X

Who Is Generation X?

Generation Xers may like to call themselves the "Why Me?" generation, but they should be called the "Whiny" generation. — David Martin in Newsweek[1]

Ever since *Time* discovered the "twentysomething generation" in the summer of 1990, almost every major cultural institution — From Taco Bell to the Clinton campaign — has tried to devise a twentysomething contraption of its own. — Alexander Star in *The New Republic*[2]

When I first heard the phrase "Generation X," I thought it was in reference to a new generation of black youth who were moved to thought, dialogue, and action by Spike Lee's 1992 cinematic production of the slain human-civil rights leader Malcolm X. I was appalled to learn that the phrase is actually a media-generated, -fabricated, and -propagated label for the post-baby boom generation (ages 18-30). — Darrell Armstrong in *Sojourners*[3]

We're kind of an after-thought generation. The spotlight is on the Boomers and the old people. We're basically ignored. — Jeff Bailey in *Baby Busters*[4]

The generation's attitude has been summed up by the media in a single word: "slacker." — David Lipsky and Alexander Abrams in *Harpers Magazine*[5]

Generation X and Their Place In History

Generation X? Twentysomething? Baby Buster? 13th Gen? You may be in the dark concerning these references. Just exactly who are these people? Those are just some of the names and labels that have been given to the generation of children born between the years of 1961-1981.[6] Actually, there isn't even any agreement on that. George Barna, of the Barna

Research Group, wants to make the break from 1965 to 1983. He refers to them as "Baby Busters" and his reason for doing so is ". . . because the era from 1965 through 1983 produced fewer babies per year than were born during the Boom years — i.e., there was a birth bust."[7] Geoffrey Holtz, in *Welcome to the Jungle: The Why Behind "Generation X"*, chooses 1960 for the beginning date of Generation X. He argues that this was the year that the G. D. Searle Drug Company first offered the birth control pill to the public. This made it so much easier *not* to have children and was the beginning of the "baby bust" years.[8] Others have suggested that 1963 is the defining year for the beginning of Generation X because on November 22 of that year John F. Kennedy was assassinated. Up until this time the tone of the nation and of every generation that had preceded them was one of optimism. Things will get better. There is always hope. But with the fall of "Camelot" came the dark years. Youthful optimism and hope died. A pervading spirit of cynicism, negativity and apathy took its place. Such was the world into which the first Xers were born.

But there is really no need or profit in arguing over the difference of a few years. The members of Generation X are not defined as much by chronology as they are by attitude and outlook. There is some crossover to be found between the Boomers and the Busters. You might know someone who fits the personality and characteristics of a Boomer who was born in 1965, while at the same time knowing someone who was born in 1960 who is a typical Buster through and through.

GENERATION	BIRTH YEARS	AGE IN 1996
Lost	1883-1900	96-113
G.I.	1901-1924	72-95
Silent	1925-1942	54-71
Boom	1943-1960	36-53
Generation X	1961-1981	15-35
Millennial	1982- ?	0-14
		Source: *Generations*

Barna offers a slightly modified version of the previous table. He identifies the generation born in 1926 and earlier as "Seniors." Those who were born from 1927 to 1945 he calls "Builders." "Boomers" he places in the years from 1946 to 1964. "Busters" are those born in 1965 to 1983. He does not yet have a label for those born in 1984 to the present.[9]

Labels, Labels, Labels

A few years back there was a commercial on TV by the Libby's corporation that portrayed a scene where a child was watching his mother prepare dinner. As she was opening a can of vegetables the child's eyes lit up and he broke into singing this little ditty, "If it says, Libby's, Libby's, Libby's on the label, label, label, I will like it, like it, like it, on the table, table, table." Well, liking labels might be okay in helping you identify quality canned vegetables, but most people resent labels being attached to them and find labeling to be unfair. So it is with Generation X. They hate labels with a passion. Especially the ones that have been assigned to their generation. Who can blame them? Consider some of the negative labels and descriptions that the media has tagged them with. "The Doofus Generation" (*The Washington Post*); "The Tuned-Out Generation" (*Time*); "A Generation of Animals" (*The Washington Post*); "The Numb Generation" (*The New York Times*); "The Blank Generation" (*The San Francisco Examiner*); "The Unromantic Generation" (*The New York Times*).[10]

> My generation has been called various things by our elders, not many of them positive. We have been described as lazy, useless, ill-educated and shallow. We are considered a Peter Pan generation, unwilling to grow up, slow to start careers and launch families. We are defined in contrast to the generation that immediately preceded us — and that likes us least — the Baby Boomers. In their eyes they are the world's boom and we its bust. Thus we are called the "Baby Busters." We have also been called "Generation X" because it was thought that we stand for nothing and believe in nothing.[11]

21

Picking up on the negativity associated with most of the labels, Howe and Strauss tried to give them a non-label label by giving them a number instead. Thirteen. They refer to them as the 13th Gen because this is the thirteenth generation to be born since the writing of the Constitution. But this is not much help. I mean, thirteen? What a bummer of a number! That is the universal symbol for bad luck. Buildings don't have a thirteenth floor, airplanes don't have a thirteenth row and nobody wants to drive a race car with the number thirteen. Who can forget Friday the 13th? There just has to be something better.

Actually, in the early '70s some more positive labels were suggested. "Computer Babies" or "High-Tech Generation" was considered for a while. These labels seemed to hint at the technological changes and advances that would be so much a part of this generation. Some commentators suggested the "Scarce Generation" in reference to the low birth rate. It was thought that this would be an advantage for the members of this generation because the lack of numbers would mean less competition for good jobs and career choice. (Unfortunately the opposite seems to have occurred anyway). *Fortune* magazine called them the "Upbeat Generation" because of their "no problem" attitude. But for all the good intentions of what might have been, downbeat and negative labels seem to be the norm.

We've been called "baby bummers," "twenty-nothings," "slackers," "the Repair Generation," "the Surviving Generation" and "the Generation After." We've been defined by demographics, time frames, societal trends, behavior, attitudes and the price of our sneakers. We've been called selfish, lazy, shallow, image-conscious, indifferent, unmotivated, apathetic, nihilistic, disenfranchised, angry and angst-ridden.[12]

Do you hear the frustration and the anger behind that quotation? While labels may be an inevitable part of life, and especially for those in the media, if you ever want to reach an Xer you will have to do it without labels. When someone tries to put a label on them, they interpret that as an attempt to gain a superior and more powerful position over them. They don't like being in the "one-down" position. So when you are working with this generation, go out of your way to try to treat each person as unique, valuable and having potential. Let them speak for themselves. It may be that they share many common characteristics, but don't just assume. Allow them the chance to speak and act on their own behalf and then respond accordingly.

Having said that they hate labels, for the purposes of this book, I am still stuck with the unpleasant task of using one, if only for the purposes of identification and discussion. I am choosing to use the term Generation X or Xer. This term was first coined by Douglas Coupland in his 1991 novel *Generation X: Tales for an Accelerated Culture*. It was quickly picked up by the media and interpreted to mean that this was a generation characterized as being "without anything." They had no distinctive voice, goals, music or identity. They were the unknown factor. While some of this generation preferred this label to the others because it at least paid ". . . homage to this generation's disdain for accepting any single definition,"[13] I am using it for several different reasons. First, in mathematics, X is the unknown factor in algebraic equations that helps you solve the problem and find the solution. I see great potential and possibilities for this generation. They could represent the vanguard of great new changes and ideas, both for society and the church. The solutions to many of society's ills may lie within this generation. What is needed is some nurturing, encouragement and support.

Secondly, X is the equivalent of the Greek letter *chi* which was sometimes used as an abbreviation for *Christos* or Christ. If this generation is going to triumph over the myriad of individual, family and societal problems that have been dropped on their front door step, they will need the transforming and healing power of Jesus. Let them be identified with the one who also knows what it is like to be rejected by family, society and friends (Is 53:3; Matt 13:53-58; 27:20-26; Jn 7:3-5; 1 Pet 2:4).

Thirdly, there isn't a kid in the world who doesn't know the meaning and value of an "X" marked on a treasure map. "X" marks the spot where the buried treasure is hidden! I believe that within every Xer is hidden treasure. Within them lies talent, compassion, gifts and dreams just waiting to be discovered. This is especially true of those who have named Christ as their personal Lord and Savior. It is written in 2 Corinthians 4:7: "But we have this treasure in jars of clay to show that this all-surpassing power is from God and not from us."

It was customary in ancient times to hide valuable items such as silver, gold and jewels in clay jars. This was done because the clay jars, being very plain and having little outward worth or beauty, did not attract attention to themselves or the treasures that were contained within them. So it is with many members of Generation X. Their weird haircuts and clothing styles may turn people off outwardly, but hiding underneath it all lies a wealth of untapped potential and unrecognized treasure. The world, and especially the church, needs to look beyond the outer facade and learn to appreciate them for what they have to offer the world and to look for the treasure that lies within.

What's In A Name, Anyway?

Remember the little song that you were taught to sing in childhood if someone called you a name? "Sticks and stones can break my bones, but words can never hurt me." Who thought up that song, anyway? They must have been brain dead because every adult knows that words have power and they *can* hurt. They can hurt for a long time. If you don't believe this, just talk to someone who was given an undesirable childhood nickname like "four-eyes," "carrot-top," "fatty," or "stupid." They will assure you that the sting of those words reaches far into adulthood and much of what they do or don't do today is an attempt to overcome the pain from those memories.

Names are important. In western culture names have lost

some of their significance. They have simply become a means of identification and no more. But in ancient cultures, and with Israel especially, names were looked upon as an expression of one's essential character, the essence of personality and the expression of the innermost being. A change in name usually accompanied a change in character.

The Talmud stated that "among the four things that cancel the doom of a man is change of name (RH 16b)."[14] The belief in the power of a name was so important to the people of the Middle Ages that they developed the custom of changing or giving an additional name to the name of a person who was dangerously ill, or who suffered some other misfortune in the belief that the angel of death would be confused as a result of the new name.

A name in the Old Testament was either descriptive of the parent's wishes or prophetic of the personality of the one who was being named. A name was considered to be an integral part of a person's character and fortune. If you search through the Old Testament you will find about a dozen examples where a person's name was changed. In every one of these the change in name symbolized the introduction of a new relation- ship, a new quality of character, a new phase of life, or perhaps a new vocation. Knowing the name of a person was equivalent to knowing his essence. To change the name of a person was to imply a change in the character and mission of that person.[15]

People have a remarkable propensity for living up to other's expectations of them. If "slacker," "doofus," "numb and dumb" is the label that you stick on this next generation, then don't be surprised at what you get. It would be wiser and more prof- itable to look for positive and encouraging words to say. We need to heed the words of Paul who said, "Do not let any unwholesome talk come out of your mouths, but only what is helpful for building others up according to their needs, that it may benefit those who listen" (Eph 4:29). This is especially true for Generation X.

Life Application and Implication For Ministry

1. Ask your children or youth group members if they have heard of any labels attached to their generation. If so, what are they? What do they understand them to mean? Seek to discover and understand their response to them.
2. Were most of the labels positive or negative? What can individual members of Generation X do to help improve their collective image? Or is the problem with those who are doing the labeling, not those who are being labeled?
3. If they could choose a different name for their generation, what would it be? Brainstorm through some new alternatives. You might adopt one as a name for your youth group and have it printed up on T-shirts.
4. Try to be aware of how much labeling you see in the media and in the world around you, whether it be at school, home or work. Make an effort to give people a chance to prove themselves on their own merits rather than pre-judging them on the basis of a whole group.
5. What insights does Matthew 7:1-5 give to this issue?

Notes

1. David Martin, "The Whiny Generation," *Newsweek*, November 1, 1993, 10.

2. Alexander Star, "The Twentysomething Myth," *The New Republic*, January 4 & 11, 1993, 22.

3. Darrell Armstrong, "The Fire Within," *Sojourners*, November 1994, 18.

4. George Barna, *Baby Busters: The Disillusioned Generation* (Chicago: Northfield Publishing, 1992), 19.

5. David Lipsky and Alexander Abrams, "The Packaging (and Re-Packaging) of a Generation," *Harpers Magazine*, July 1994, 20.

6. William Strauss & Neil Howe, *Generations: The History of America's Future, 1584 to 2069* (New York: Quill, 1991), 32.

7. Barna, *Baby Busters*, 14-15.

8. Geoffrey T. Holtz, *Welcome to the Jungle*, 2.

9. Barna, *Baby Busters*, 14.

10. Holtz, *Welcome to the Jungle*, 1.

11. William Mahedy and Janet Bernardi, *A Generation Alone: Xers Making a Place in the World* (Downers Grove: InterVarsity Press, 1994), 10.

12. Kevin Graham Ford, *Jesus For A New Generation: Putting the Gospel in the Language of Xers* (Downers Grove: InterVarsity Press, 1995), 19.

13. Holtz, *Welcome to the Jungle*, 3.

14. *Encyclopaedia Judaica*, 2nd ed., s.v. "Name, Change of."

15. See *The Zondervan Pictorial Encyclopedia of the Bible*, 4th ed., s.v. "Name" and *The Interpreter's Dictionary of the Bible*, 1st ed., s.v. "Name."

Unwanted: Dead or Alive

When they were born, they were the first babies people took pills not to have. — Howe and Strauss in *13th Gen: Abort, Retry, Ignore, Fail?*[1]

In the seventies and early eighties, 70 to 90 percent of all newly constructed apartments in large cities such as Dallas, Houston, and Denver were strictly adults-only. — Geoffrey T. Holtz in *Welcome to the Jungle: The Why Behind "Generation X"*[2]

Babies are the enemy. Not your baby or mine, of course. Individually they are all cute. But together they are a menace. — John Sommerville in *The Rise and Fall of Childhood*[3]

At some point society's treatment of the young had shifted from nurture to hostility. — William Mahedy and Janet Bernardi in *A Generation Along: Xers Making a Place in the World.*[4]

Each American baby represents fifty times as great a threat to the planet as each Indian baby. — *Life*[5]

The Birth Control Factor

From time to time in the old west, wanted posters would be hung up around the town. They would have a picture of some desperado on them and beneath the picture would be the price of the reward offered for the capture of the criminal along with the conditions; "Wanted: Dead or Alive." It certainly wasn't a desirable situation to be in, but at least they were wanted. Generation X was unwanted: dead or alive. I am referring to the popular use of the birth control pill to prevent conception and the millions of abortions that took place every year to put an end to the unwanted pregnancies.

There have been attempts at birth control from ancient times. Families didn't always "plan" on having that new arrival, but when it took place there was usually great joy surrounding a healthy birth and lots of attention given to the infant by family, friends and siblings. The introduction of the birth control pill in 1960 changed all of that. Never was it so easy and so effective to *not* have children. Not only did this cause a national drop in the birth rate which continued over several years, but it changed the nation's attitude towards children. A pervading spirit of hostility towards children silently crept into the nation's housing laws, politics and movies. The message was clear. Children were unwanted. "Fueled by the hostile environment toward children, the number of young couples who remained childless during these years swelled to 75% (the term actually mutated from "childless" to "child-free")."[6]

> Four years after it was first made available. . . the first oral contraceptive was already used regularly by 10 percent of married couples. And the numbers rose steadily until, by 1980, one fourth of women of reproductive age were relying on the pill. In the most extreme development of birth control, over a million Americans a year had themselves surgically sterilized during the seventies, a procedure that was almost unheard of just a decade earlier. During the seventies 10 million people made sure that they would never have another child. America's love affair with its children was, at least for now, a thing of the past.[7]

The syndicated columnist, Ann Landers, ran a survey in 1975. She asked for parents to respond to the question, "If you had to do it all over again, would you have had children?" From among the thousands of replies that she received in response to her question 70% answered "No!"[8] Even those kids who *were* truly wanted by their parents still had a rough row to hoe because they had to learn to deal with a world that was unusually hostile to the interests of children.

Abortion

The 13th is the most aborted generation in American history. After rising sharply during the late 1960s and early 1970s, the abortion rate climbed by another 80 percent during the first six years (1973 to 1979) after the Supreme Court's *Roe* v. *Wade* decision. Through the birth years of last-wave 13ers, would-be mothers aborted one fetus in three.[9]

The hostility towards children took a chilling turn in 1973 with the legalization of abortion. Now it was outright war. The number of casualties is staggering. If you add up all of the casualties from the combined wars of the United States beginning with the Revolutionary War and going all the way to the Vietnam War, the total number would be 1,296,081 war dead.[10] Since the *Roe* v. *Wade* decision of 1973 an average of 1,500,000 legalized abortions have been performed per year.[11] ". . . across the country unborn children are being aborted at a rate exceeding 4,000 every day."[12] Lest you deceive yourself and make an erroneous assumption that this wholesale slaughter is only being carried out by those outside the church, you should know that "One out of every six women who have an abortion claims to be an evangelical. The rate is even higher among Catholic women."[13]

WAR	CASUALTIES	WAR	CASUALTIES
Revolutionary War	25,324	War on the unborn since 1973 through the end of 1996 based on averages	1,500,000 per year for twenty-three years
Civil War	498,332		
World War I	116,516		
World War II	545,108		
Korean War	54,246		
Vietnam War	56,555		
TOTAL	**1,296,081**	**TOTAL**	**34,500,000**
		Source: *Abortion: The Silent Holocaust*	

Zero Population Growth

After the baby boom, America began to reevaluate its attitudes towards children. A number of books were written which warned about a catastrophe in the making if the population growth rate went unchecked. Paul Ehrlich, a biologist from Stanford University, wrote a book entitled *The Population Bomb* in which he predicted food shortages, riots, starvation, and one and a half billion people perishing worldwide from disease, starvation and other related problems due to overpopulation. To keep this horror from happening, Ehrlich suggested a number of baby-prevention measures: luxury taxes on cribs, diapers, and expensive toys; "responsibility prizes" awarded to each couple for every five years they remained childless; and a "special lottery" with tickets going only to the childless.[14]

To help educate and discourage people from having children, Ehrlich founded an organization called "Zero Population Growth, Inc." ZPG grew rapidly with a membership of over 700,000 by the eighties.

A number of solutions were suggested to stem the population explosion. One economist wanted governmental licensing of children. Senator Bob Packwood proposed removing the tax exemption for any child beyond the second. The most extreme measure was suggested by a Tufts Medical School professor who wanted to put fertility-depressing drugs in municipal water supplies. Even though none of these suggestions were actually carried out, they set the nation's mood. The message was clear: "Kids are not welcome here."

Latchkey Kids

Many of the children who did manage to make their entrance into the world found that they were on their own at a very young age. Generation X suffered from neglect at the hands of parents who placed career and the accumulation of things ahead of the responsibilities of parenthood. Boomer parents were bound and determined that their children would not become a hindrance to their career advancement and the fulfillment of their dreams. Mothers went back to work as soon as they could. Infants were left with sitters. Toddlers were warehoused in day-care and school-age children were given a key on a string and the responsibility for their own welfare for anywhere from two to four hours a day. It was up to them to get home, unlock the door, feed and entertain themselves until mom or dad got home. You could easily identify dozens of these kids on the playgrounds of America's schools. They all wore the ever-present key on a string around their necks. The term "latchkey kids" was coined to identify this new phenomenon. Thomas Long, of the Catholic University of America, estimated there were up to 10 million latchkey children under the age of 14 across the nation.[15] One-fourth of these kids lived in constant fear. They were not just a little scared, but were petrified — terrorized. These children went home every day to empty houses with no one to supervise their activities or care for their needs should they get sick or injured. Some concerned communities set up special hot-lines for latchkey kids to call if they got lonely or needed help. Many kids would call the hotline everyday just to check in with a surrogate "grandpa" or "grandma." They sorely missed the comforting presence of a caring adult. Mom and dad were needed, whether they believed it or not.

Working Mothers

Working Mothers as a Percent of All Mothers				
	1960	1970	1980	1990
With children under age 6	20%	32%	47%	60%
With children age 6-17	43%	51%	64%	76%
Source: *U.S. Bureau of Labor Statistics*				

Influenced by the rising tide of militant feminism and the belief that children were not a valid reason for not having a career, many women abandoned their traditional role as the chief nurturer and entered the marketplace. Those mothers who wanted to stay at home and who had no desire to pursue a career were often made to feel guilty, inadequate and undervalued for their choice. Motherhood and homemaking was not a "real job." The stay-home mother became a relic of the past. In 1960 the percent of working mothers with children under the age of six was 20%. For those with children ages six to seventeen the figure increased to 43%. By 1980 those figures jumped to 47% and 64% respectively. 1990 saw an all time high of 60 and 76% for those same categories.[16] As a result of this migration the proportion of preschoolers cared for in their own homes fell by half. By the late seventies and early eighties 39% of those mothers with infants under the age of one were working.[17] This loss of time spent together has far-reaching upon the child which may not show up until later years.

> Dr. Burton White of the Harvard University Preschool Project concluded that "what happens between 0-18 months of life does more to influence future intellectual competence than any other time." White's data also concluded that the nuclear family is the most important education system.

> Children who receive inadequate nurture in their early years become nonattached. According to Selma Fraiberg of the University of Michigan, nonattachment, at its worst, can "create bondless people who. . . contribute far beyond their number to social disease and disorder. They are handicapped in work relationships, friendships, marriage, and child rearing."[18]

When mom went off to work, some children were left with their grandparents or personal sitters. The majority, however, were placed in day-care. "The evidence shows that children cared for by someone other than one of their parents during their preschool years had more behavioral problems in school at ten years old than their non-day-care peers."[19] What kind of care did most of these children receive in these centers? In the summer of 1970, the National Council of Jewish Women visited 431 licensed and unlicensed day-care centers across the country. These day-care centers were responsible for the oversight and care of approximately 24,000 children. How did they rate these centers?

Of those centers that were for profit, only 1 percent were rated as "superior" and another 15 percent as "good." Another 35 percent were considered "fair" — indicated that they provided only custodial care — and *half* were rated as "poor." The non-profit centers, typically government- or church-supported, were better, but half were still only considered "fair" and 10 percent were "poor."[20]

All of this took its toll on the children. Job demands added extra stress to family life. It ate up time that would have been spent in one-on-one interaction and nurturing. After a long, hard day at the office, most parents want to rest and relax. They don't have the physical or emotional energy to play with the kids, help them with their homework or answer their questions. According to Harvard psychiatrist Armand Nicholi, American parents spend less time with their children than do parents in any other country of the world.[21]

Housing Laws

In the seventies and early eighties a high percentage of newly constructed apartment complexes were designated as strictly adults-only. In some large cities, such as Dallas, Houston, and Denver the percentages were as high as 70% to 90%.[22] A study conducted in 1979 found that seven apartment complexes out of ten excluded children.[23] With the trend across the nation leaning towards the exclusion of children in the new housing units, that left the older and poorer quality ones for families. Because of the lack of available housing for families and the simple laws of supply and demand, families with children had to pay a higher price for their housing.

Renters who were childless when they signed their lease were given eviction notices upon the arrival of a new baby. One might think that would be impossible in America. You should be able to live where you want. What about The Fair Housing Act, passed by Congress in 1968 and amended in 1974? It prohibited the discrimination in the sale or rental of housing on the basis of race, color, religion, sex or national origin. Other legislation covered the rights of the elderly. But there was nothing that protected the rights of families with children. Not until 1988 did Congress amend the Civil Rights Act of 1968 and make discrimination against families with children illegal.[24]

Movies, Restaurants and the Swinging Single

In the years preceding Generation X, children were portrayed in a very positive and likable way. Who wasn't drawn to the charm and antics of "The Little Rascals?" Shirley Temple won people's hearts in *The Good Ship Lollipop* and other feature films. Disney created the child-star Haley Mills.

The children of Generation X were not so lucky. The late sixties and seventies and mid-eighties saw Hollywood develop a whole new genre of "evil children" movies. It started with *Rosemary's Baby*, *The Exorcist*, *Carrie*, and *The Omen* and ended with *Firestarter* and *Children of the Corn*.[25]

These movies only worked to further promote the notion that children were evil, bad and undesirable. Many had Satanic and occult themes to them. It was as if the producers were trying to make a case for children being "the spawn of the devil."

Movies were not the only place where the public removed the welcome mat from underneath the feet of children. Unlike the '50s or '90s, a parent entering a restaurant in the '70s with a little child was commonly met with no high chair, no children's menu, and disapproving glances from waiters and patrons. The implied message was, "We came to enjoy a meal out as a couple. Leave your screaming brat at home. Why should our meal be spoiled by your undisciplined and unruly kid?"

Interest in parenting went down. "*Parents* magazine saw its circulation plummet from 2.1 million in 1971 to 1.4 million in 1979, a 33 percent drop."[26] This drop could not be explained by the zero population growth influence because the actual *number* of parents went up slightly in the seventies. The most logical explanation for this decline was a decline in the interest in parenting, reflecting once again, the general tone of the nation.

Children born to parents in the Gen X years were no longer viewed as the number one priority for gaining happiness as they had been in the years before. "By the early eighties they had dropped to number four. Right behind automobiles."[27]

The developing singles scene also put a damper on the thought of marriage and raising a family. Record numbers of adults simply chose to postpone or forgo marriage. They were having too good of a time at the singles bars and discos. The spoiled Boomers just refused to grow up. They wanted to remain the eternal adolescent. Having a kid would only "cramp their style." They wanted to be free of any responsibilities connected with child raising to pursue their own selfish interests.

The national "welcome wagon" stayed parked in the garage for the arrival of Generation X. Unwanted, unheralded, and unwelcome, Generation X had to make their own way. They quickly learned how to harden themselves in order to deal with the rejection and they became the authorities on how to become "a survivor."

Along with this survivor mentality came an underlying rage and resentment. It can best be understood by a trendy national phenomenon which took place in the late '80s. All over the country little yellow warning signs with the words "Baby On Board" began to appear in the rear windows of our automobiles. It represented a 180 degree turn in the nation's attitude towards children. While Generation X was aborted and abandoned in record numbers, these little signs were the heralds of a new spirit blowing through the country. It was a spirit of nurture and caring. It pleaded with the world, "Please be careful around me because I have precious cargo inside — my baby."

This sickened and enraged the members of Generation X. They wanted to know "Why this change in attitude?" "How come we weren't wanted?" Why weren't we treated as precious cargo?" "What did we ever do to deserve the neglect and abuse we received from your hands, while this generation is loved, cared for and adored?" For generations preceding them and for the one after them, children were loved and wanted. All of them except their generation. Generation X — the kids nobody wanted.

Life Application and Implication For Ministry

1. If you are the parent of an Xer, make a special effort to reassure every one of your children that they are wanted. Explain to them that even though a child may have been "unplanned" they are still very much loved and "wanted." Be sure to do this verbally. Do not assume that they know it if you haven't said it. They need to hear it and will really appreciate it, even if they don't tell you so to your face.

2. Develop a theology of birth control. When, if ever, is it a responsible thing to do? When does it become the manifestation of a selfish spirit and a lack of responsibility towards future generations?

3. What are you and your church doing to offer the community an alternative to abortion? Do you support your local Right to Life and Birthright? If not, why not? If there isn't a local chapter in your community, pray about the possibility of sponsoring one.

4. Take of group of volunteers to your local abortion alternative center and offer your time in the way of office help, telephone calls, counseling training, solicitation of donations or passing out tracts.

5. Have the members of your youth group, Bible study or Sunday School class read Frank Peretti's book, *Tilly*, and then adapt it into a play. Present the play for an evening worship service or youth meeting.

6. In what ways could your church or youth group help with the plight of latchkey kids in your area? Could you offer an

after-school program at least one day a week which would provide tutoring, games, a Bible lesson and a snack? Have your older teens brainstorm ideas on how they could make this dream a reality.

7. If you work with youth, take a moment and evaluate how "user friendly" your church and youth programs are.

Place an "X" in the box which best describes your youth program	☺	😐	☹	💀
1. There is always someone at the door to greet visitors and guide them to a class or a vacant seat.				
2. You and your youth staff know all of your regular attenders by name; first and last.				
3. A new visitor gets a follow-up call or card within two weeks of attending a service or special event.				
4. If someone has missed several Sundays, they receive a call or card informing them that their absence was noticed.				
5. Your group is not "cliquish" and visitors are made to feel welcome and comfortable within your class or group.				

Notes

1. Neil Howe and Bill Strauss, *13th Gen*, 13.

2. Geoffrey T. Holtz, *Welcome to the Jungle*, 10.

3. John Sommerville, *The Rise and Fall of Childhood* (New York: Vintage Books, 1982), 7.

4. William Mahedy and Janet Bernardi, *A Generation Alone*, 22.

5. "Squeezing Into the '70s," *Life*, 9 January 1970, 8.

6. Holtz, *Welcome to the Jungle*, 18.

7. Ibid., 19.

8. Ibid., 20.

9. William Strauss and Neil Howe, *Generations*, 324.

10. John Powell, *Abortion: The Silent Holocaust* (Allen, TX: Argus Communications, 1981), i.

11. Robert Famighetti, ed., *The World Almanac and Book of Facts* (Mahwah, NJ: St. Martin's Press, 1995), 959, and John Powell, *Abortion: The Silent Holocaust*, 170.

12. Harold O. J. Brown, "Abortion Stats In Perspective," *Current Thoughts & Trends*, 11 June 1995, 20.

13. "Abortion In the Church," *Current Thoughts & Trends*, 11 January 1995, 30.

14. Paul R. Ehrlich, *The Population Bomb* (New York: Random House, 1968), 132.

15. "Perils Cited for Latchkey Children," *Youthletter*, March 1986, 3.

16. U.S. Bureau of Labor Statistics, quoted in Howe and Strauss, 58.

17. Holtz, *Welcome to the Jungle*, 40.

18. "Empty Houses, Empty Children," *Current Thoughts & Trends*, 10, August 1994, 13.

19. "Day Care Detriment." *Current Thoughts & Trends*, 11 November 1995, 12.

20. Ibid., 43.

21. Mark DeVries, *Family-Based Youth Ministry: Reaching the Been-There, Done-That Generation* (Downers Grove: InterVarsity, 1994), 40.

22. Richard Louv, *Childhood's Future: Listening to the American Family. New Hope for the Next Generation* (Boston: Houghton Mifflin, 1990), 311-312.

23. Margaret C. Simms, *Families and Housing Markets: Obstacles to Locating Suitable Housing* (HUD, 1980), 41.

24. "Adults-Only Housing Hears the Pitter Patter of Little Feet." *Business Week*, 13 March 1989.

25. For a complete list of the films and their release dates see Howe and Strauss, 66.

26. Holtz, *Welcome to the Jungle*, 20.

27. Ibid., 21.

Dysfunction Junction

Researchers who analyzed 11,000 separate crimes committed in three different urban areas concluded there was no clear link between crime and poverty or between crime and race. There was, however, a strong correlation with "father absent- households." — *Current Thoughts and Trends*[1]

It's not that we're whiny. We're cynical and isolated. I, for one, had a hard time trusting anything: Love is forever (my parents divorced when I was 4). — Piper Lowell in *Sojourners*[2]

"I am homesick for the home I've never had" screams out the lead singer for the rock group Soul Asylum on their hit song "Homesick." — Andres Tapia in *Christianity Today*[3]

He who attacks marriage, who undermines by word or by action this foundation of all moral society, is my enemy. Marriage is the Alpha and Omega of civilization. It makes the savage gentle, and the gentility of the most civilized finds its highest expression in marriage. — Johann Goethe (1749-1832)[4]

Unless you have men civilizing boys, guiding and disciplining them — and an idea of manhood that includes fatherhood — you are putting the foundation of your civilization at risk. — William Bennett in *Current Thoughts & Trends*[5]

When I first read the words of President Theodore Roosevelt on the importance of fatherhood and motherhood, they sounded very much like a prophecy concerning the plight of Generation X. It was as if he was able to see beyond his time into the future and foresee the devastating effects that parental neglect was going to have on an entire generation of young people. Listen as he speaks. His words will haunt you.

There are exceptional women, there are exceptional men, who have other tasks to perform in addition to the task of mother-hood and fatherhood, the task of providing for the home and of keeping it. But it is the tasks connected with the home that are the fundamental tasks of humanity. . . . if the mother does not do her duty, there will either be no next generation, or a next generation that is worse than none at all. . . .[6]

I am in complete agreement with the keen insight of Presi-dent Roosevelt. As I have shared with the kids in my youth groups and college classes, and listened to their stories as they have poured their hearts out, I am convinced that nothing has so deeply affected the lives of Generation X or caused them as much pain as their own family life. Or perhaps it would be more correctly stated, the lack of a family life.

No other American generation has ever grown up in families of such complexity. In 1980, just 56 percent of all dependent chil-dren lived with two once-married parents, another 14 percent with at least one previously married parent, 11 percent with a stepparent, and 19 percent with one parent. One in five had half siblings.[7]

Divorce and Dysfunction

The children of Generation X have experienced the trauma of divorce in record numbers. "Between 1965 and 1977, when the busters were born, the numbers of both divorces and out-of-wedlock births doubled. As a result, 40% of today's young adults have spent at least some time in a single-parent family by age 16."[8] In 1961, at the beginning of the Gen X era, there were 375,000 divorces involving a half-million children, a statis-tic that had remained fairly constant through the previous decades. Just ten years later, into the heart of the Gen X years, the yearly rate had risen to 650,000 divorces affecting nearly a million children. By 1975 the nation saw a million marriages dis-solved involving more than 1.1 million children. This same rate of disintegration has continued up through the present so that it is estimated than more than 40% of the members of

42

Generation X are children of divorce, compared to only 11% of those born during the fifties.[9]

A partial explanation for the increase in the number of divorces was the changing attitude about divorce and children. In years past parents in bad marriages believed that it was best to stay together for the sake of the kids. That all changed for Generation X.

> In 1962, half of all adult women believed that parents in bad marriages should stay together for the sake of the children; by 1980, only one in five thought so. A 13er child in the 1980s faced twice the risk of parental divorce as a boomer child in the mid-1960s — and three times the risk a Silent child faced back in 1950. Four-fifths of today's divorced adults profess to being happier afterward, but a majority of their children feel otherwise.[10]

The "wisdom" of the psychological and sociological experts of the time assured parents that getting a divorce was much better for the kids in the long run than having them grow up in the midst of conflict and frustration. Parents were told that children were resilient and could survive any crisis with little adverse affects. The only problem is that the experts failed to ask the kids how they felt. Overwhelmingly, kids had a negative response to their parents' decision to split up. If they were given the choice between an intact family with all its problems and a divorced family with its lack of strife, the majority of kids would choose the intact family. "Less than 10 percent report being relieved by their parents' divorce — and those children who do feel relieved still seem to have difficulty adjusting to the divorce."[11] Because they have suffered the brunt of the divorce epidemic, 79% of Xers think that America's divorce laws are too lenient. Only 2% think they are about right and 15% believe that they are not easy enough.[12]

> One of the major reasons Baby Busters are the most pessimistic generation in our nation's history is that they have felt the sting of divorce more than any prior generation. More than half of them lived in a family that went through a divorce, and more than four out of five had close friends whose parents split up.

These experiences have colored their fears about their own future.[13]

One of the most noticeable ways that divorce hurt growing Xers was economically. The majority of them stayed with their mothers after the divorce. Divorce usually meant a significant loss of income for the mother. "One study, for example, found that income for mothers and children declined on average about 30 percent, while fathers experienced a 10 to 15 percent increase in income in the year following a separation."[14] This loss of income usually involved a move to more inexpensive living quarters also. Sometimes this meant moving to a different town or state so they also lost their friends and familiar surroundings.

The Effects of Divorce

Research makes clear that children suffer greatly when parents decide to split up. Children of divorce generally receive less care and discipline from the remaining parent, are less adept at play with schoolmates, suffer from worse health, have a greater tendency to exhibit emotional and sexual problems as well as anti-social behavior, have a more negative outlook on the world, and lack any identification with role models. They are likely to be chronically unhappy; to feel a deep sense of loneliness and rejection; and to crave structure in their lives.[15]

The negative effects of the divorce upon Generation X lasted years beyond the event itself. More than a third of them experienced moderate or severe depression up to five years after the divorce. Ten years after the divorce they are leading lives that are characterized as troubled, drifting, and under-achieving. Even fifteen years later they still feel the effects upon their own lives as they struggle to establish strong love relationships of their own.

The epidemic divorce rate also contributed to the dramatic increase in crime. "Nationally, more than 70 percent of all juveniles in state reform institutions come from fatherless homes."[16] Several studies have been done which controlled factors such as race and income in the analysis. What these studies found was that boys from single-mother homes were significantly more likely than others to commit crimes and wind up in juvenile court and penitentiary systems. Time and time again it was proven that the breakup of the family was a much more significant factor in the prediction of involvement in juvenile crime than either low income or race.

The performance drop of Generation X in education has received national attention. Surely there are a number of contributing factors involved in this phenomenon, and many of these will be addressed later. But it must be considered that one of the reasons for their poor performance is ". . . not because they are intellectually or physically impaired but because they are emotionally incapacitated."[17] Teachers across the nation have attested to the dramatic increase in acting-out behavior in the classroom, especially in boys from single-parent families.

The effect of divorce on the members of Generation X could be summarized in the following chart. For years to come our nation will continue to reap the consequences of our divorce-happy, narcissistic society. We already see it in the widespread teenage depression, rising crime rates, suicide rates, relational crises, moral ambiguity, the lack of socialization skills and a general breakdown in the very fabric of society. The only positive thing that can be said about it is that it has made Xers bound and determined not to make the same mistakes

---

The Effects of Divorce on Generation X

- They express feelings of sadness, neediness and a sense of their own vulnerability.
- They speak sorrowfully of their loss of an intact family and the lack of opportunity for a close relationship with their fathers.
- They are anxious about relationships with the opposite sex, marriage and personal commitments.
- They fear betrayal, hurt and abandonment in relationships.
- Teenage girls who experienced a divorce as children are more likely to become involved in dating and sexual relationships than guys.
- Teenage guys are more lonely and wary of relationships.

Source: *The Youth Ministry Resource Book*

---

with their families. "My generation will be the family genera-tion. . . . I don't want my kids to go through what my parents put me through."[18]

Blended Families

Not only were large numbers of Xers subjected to the prob-lems and pain of a parental divorce, but a sizable amount of those had to go through the trials of learning how to adjust to the dynamics and complicated relational issues of a stepfamily. "In about one-fourth of all the weddings that take place in a given year both the bride and the groom are entering their second or subsequent marriage, but almost 50% of marriages involve at least one person who has been married previously."[19]

One would think that a stepfamily situation would be more desirable than a single-parent family because you would have pooled resources, added income, and the presence of both male and female role models for the children. From the stand-point of the single parent, remarriage does bring with it the hope of new commitments, happiness and a second chance. For them it is a blessed relief from the stress and loneliness, but the children in a blended family situation don't always share their parent's optimism.

In a study by Judith Wallerstein, nearly half the children said they felt left out in their stepfamilies.[20] On top of that, second marriages are 20% more likely than first marriages to fail, once again sending the children on an emotional roller coaster ride. In a 1986 study by Glynnis Walker on divorced families, only 14% of the children who lived in new families said they felt good about the relationship between their natural parents and their stepparents.[21] Children from stepfamilies are more likely to indicate that they often feel lonely or depressed than children from either single-parent or intact families.

Being in a new family can also adversely affect a child's rela-tionship with his/her natural parents. Listen to the words of a young girl whose father remarried: "I felt like a carry-over, a left-over from a life my father wanted to forget. Every time he looked at me, he saw my mother. . . I was a living reminder of what had failed."[22]

A large percentage of children in stepfamily situations do not even consider their stepparents to be part of their families. According to the National Survey on Children, when asked the question, "When you think of your family, who do you include?", only 10% of the children failed to mention a biological parent, even if they were separated from them, but 33% left out a stepparent. When parents were asked the same question, only one percent failed to mention a natural child, but 15% left out a stepchild.[23]

One of the most serious concerns about children in stepfamily situations is the high amount of abuse that they endure. A study by Canadian researchers Martin Daly and Margo Wilson on preschool children in stepfamilies found that these children are forty times as likely as children in intact families to suffer physical or sexual abuse. (In most of these cases the abuse was not performed by the stepfather, but by a third

---

Stepfamilies

- 1,300 new stepfamilies are formed every day in the United States.
- One in every 5 children in the United States is a stepchild.
- 60% of the children born today will spend part of their life in 1 or more step-relationships.
- More than 35 million adults are stepparents.
- 75% of all step-relationships are likely to fail, with child and step-related issues being the major reasons for failure.
- 57% of stepfamilies divorce.

Source: *The Youth Ministry Resource Book*

---

party, such as a neighbor or friend of the stepfather.)[24] Even though the stepfather was not actively involved in the abuse, the facts still confirm that stepchildren are not as well cared for as biological children.

Stepparents do not invest as much time in their stepchildren as do parents in intact families or even single-parent families.

They are less likely to become involved in a stepchild's school life, projects or to coach their athletic team.

All of this is not to say that there weren't some very good and healthy stepfamily situations for Generation X. Nor do I want it to seem that I am against stepfamilies, or think that they are all bad, adding to their burden. It is important to understand that blended families are not nuclear families. They do not automatically repair and fix what was broken with the divorce. They often bring with them their own unique sets of problems and issues to solve.[25]

Single-Parent Families

"A child in a one-parent family is only slightly more likely to live with a divorced parent as with a never-married parent, compared to ten years ago when three times as many children lived with a divorced parent as with a never-married parent."[26] Divorced people account for 37% of single parents, but the never-marrieds are not far behind with 35%. Nearly four million never-married women 18 to 44 years old have had a least one child — that's 25% of all women in that age group.[27]

Why the increase in the number of parents who have never been married? There are a number of factors involved, but most of them reflect the liberal changes in society's attitudes towards women and sexuality. With the stigma taken away from out-of-wedlock babies, more and more young girls are keeping their babies rather than giving them up for adoption or getting an abortion.

Financial rewards through additional welfare payments makes single-parenting seem like a more desirable alternative for the single girl trying to make it on her own out in the world. There are also more career opportunities available for women in today's market. They are not as dependent upon men for the financial security needed to raise a child in today's world.

The influence of radical feminism has contributed to many women choosing to start a family without the benefit of a husband. Their philosophy is, "Who needs a man, anyway?" "A single woman can do just as good a job, if not a better one, raising a child by herself as one who has a husband." Unfortunately, the children born into these situations are the ones who have to endure the consequences of this ideological tripe. Listen to the insights of sociologist David Popeno, who has devoted much of his career to the study of families. He writes:

> In three decades of work as a social scientist, I know of few other bodies of data in which the weight of evidence is so decisively on one side of the issue: on the whole, for children, two-parent families are preferable to single-parent and stepfamilies.[28]

Intact Families

While it may be true that two-parent families are preferable to single-parent families, that is not to say that they are without their own problems. Even in the families that stayed intact for Generation X, issues of career choice over family, physical and sexual abuse, drug and alcohol problems all contributed to the stress and problems of growing up an Xer.

One of the areas where parental neglect was the most obvious was in the amount of time that Boomer parents spent with their Generation X children. In the early sixties the average parents spent about 30 hours in direct contact with their children each week. By the early eighties that figure had dropped to just 17 hours. Outside of mealtimes, teenagers spend an average of only 10 minutes each day alone with their fathers — and 5 of those minutes are spent in front of the television. This is not the teen's choice. A survey of 1,200 students (ages 5-16) found that 76% wanted to spend *more* time with their parents.[29]

What difference does it make whether the parents spent a significant amount of their time involved in direct interaction with their children or not? It makes a *lot* of difference, a difference in some pretty significant areas that have ramifications on future decisions and behaviors. Research has repeatedly proven

49

that there is a strong correlation between healthy family relationships and positive social behavior in children. In Merton
and Irene Strommen's classic work, they survey 8,156 young
people and 10,467 parents. They found that teenagers who had
strong and positive relationships with their parents were more
likely to have the courage to make wise choices in the face of
peer pressure and were less likely to be involved in high-risk
behavior.[30]

Another study showed there was a strong correlation
between the amount of time that parents spent with their
teenage children and their teenagers' ability to resist sexual
temptation. Sixty-one percent of the young people who indicated that they rarely spent time with their parents had experienced sexual contact, but only 39% of those with close family
ties who spent significant amounts of time together gave in to
sexual pressure.[31]

Family time is important. It is much more than just an
overused cliché. When children are denied the needed contact
with their parents and the adult world, the loss is real. They
develop into ill-prepared teens who are unable to meet the
challenges set before them and are more likely to make decisions that will place them at risk.

Time is related to desire. Parents who love their children will
have a desire to spend time with them and will make the time.
It comes down to motivation. Healthy, loving parents are motivated to spend time with their children because they enjoy the
contact with their children and know that their children need
the one-on-one time with them. When parents are not healthy
or motivated by the right reasons, then children's needs in this
area are neglected or abused.

Stephanie[32] was adopted. Her adoptive mother was very
needy and initiated the adoption because "she wanted someone to love her and meet her needs." When this new mother
discovered that children need much more love, care and attention than they can possibly give back when they are young, she
resented her. For as long as Stephanie can remember, every

day on her birthday her mother said to her, "This is the worst day of my life. You were the worst $5,000 investment I ever made." Stephanie is 28 years old and has been out of her parent's home a long time, but her mother *still* calls her on her birthday to remind Stephanie that her birthday represents the worst day of her mother's life. A bad investment.

Stephanie has spent most of her life apologizing for her shortcomings, for who she is, and for failing to be what her mother wanted her to be. Racked with self-doubt and low self-esteem, Stephanie has tried to find her place in the world. To this day she is wary of all authoritative females, especially those in the church because her mother was supposed to be a "good Christian woman" and all she ever did was beat Stephanie down, both emotionally and physically.

Stephanie has found a shelter in her friends. "My friends *are* my family," she says. They love her, support her, encourage her and have traveled with her along the road to healing. Her

---

Sexual Abuse

- One child in five will become a victim of sexual abuse.
- At least a fourth of all girls will be sexually molested by the age of 18. One study places that risk at greater than one in three, 38%.
- Approximately one boy in 10 will be sexually molested by age 18.

Source: *Living With Teenagers* (Oct/Nov/Dec, 1990)

"Twentysomething" worship service and friends at the church make up the highlight of her week.

Physical and Sexual Abuse

Every year 6.5 million children are harmed by a parent or other family member. In 1975 a federal study indicated that 260,000 teenagers, ages 17 or younger, ran away from home for a period of a week or more. That was triple the numbers from 1964.[33] The main reason these kids ran away from home was "trouble" with their parents. Trouble could mean anything from a minor fight to a drunken brawl. The conflict often turned into physical abuse. More than 75% of all adolescent runaways experienced abuse in their homes.

> In a study abstracted by Lynn and Voigt, the following statistics were noted. 88 percent of teens were abused by at least one birth parent, and, contrary to some studies, stepparents represented a minority of the cases. 57 percent of abuse was carried out by the birth mother, whereas 31 percent was the work of a birth father. The remainder of the abuse was carried out by siblings, grandparents, stepparents and mothers' boyfriends.[34]

Often sexual abuse was a significant factor in their decision to run away. While "incest" was a word that wasn't hardly even spoken out loud in polite society during the '50s and early '60s, it has now reached epidemic proportions and society and the church can no longer ignore it. We must acknowledge the reality of the situation, horrible as it might be, and step up efforts at education, prevention and intervention. A sizable number of Generation X has suffered from this evil. While it may be too late to stop the abuse from taking place in the life of many Xers, it is never too late to begin the healing process. Healing, wholeness and restoration must now be our goal.

Drug and Alcohol Addictions

According to the Children of Alcoholics Foundation, approximately 30 million Americans have at least one alcoholic parent. That means that one out of every eight people was raised or currently lives in an alcoholic family.[35] The average classroom of 25 will have four to six children of alcoholics.[36] Conservative estimates indicate that 55% of all family violence occurs in homes where one or both parents are alcoholics. The National Association for Children of Alcoholics sets this figure at 90%.[37]

The daughter of an alcoholic father is twice as likely as her peers to be the victim of incest. In fact, incest is so prevalent in alcoholic families that some counselors will automatically assume that female clients from alcoholic families have been sexually abused unless they learn otherwise.

Children of alcoholics are themselves three to four times as likely to become alcoholics as are their peers from nonalcoholic families. Twenty-five percent of children of alcoholics will themselves become addicted to alcohol as compared to only 10 percent of the general population.[38] If they don't become addicted to alcohol like their parents, many end up addicted to something else. Seventy percent will struggle with gambling, overeating, smoking, compulsive exercising or workaholism. Because of their background growing up, they also tend to be drawn to unhealthy relationships. Half of all children of alcoholics will marry an alcoholic.

Brent[39] despises alcohol. He grew up with it and saw what it did to his family. His parents would spend most of their time at home drunk or late at the bar on weekends. They frequently got into quarrels with one another which often turned violent. Like so many kids who were raised in alcoholic families, Brent tried to fix the problem by hiding the booze or pouring it down the kitchen sink. It didn't work, but he had to at least try something to stop the chaos and bring some peace and order to his family.

He was afraid and ashamed to invite friends over because he never knew what to expect when he got home. When his parents were sober, they were nice. But they weren't sober much.

One particular event is burned into his mind, and as with all major physical burns, it, too, has left a scar. It took place on a Saturday night when he was fourteen. His parents had gone to the bar, as usual, and were drinking. They got into a fight and his father left the bar and went home. When Brent saw that his father had returned without his mother, he eventually convinced him to go back to the bar and pick her up. He got into his father's pickup with him and drove to the local tavern. It was quite late and the parking lot was almost deserted except

53

for another pickup truck and the familiar Ford Tempo which was the family car his mother drove.

As they headed for the car their headlights suddenly shone brightly on a couple of people lying on a blanket between the two vehicles. One figure rolled under the pickup truck and the other ran half-naked around the back side of the bar. What a shock it was when he realized it was his mother.

His dad turned the truck around and drove home. When they got into the house he told Brent to pack his stuff because they were leaving. While his parents talked about divorce after that event, they never actually did split up. They did, however, try giving up the alcohol and going straight, but one or the other would eventually have a relapse and end up drinking again.

While Brent's family remained intact, it was never what you could call "healthy," and Brent is still feeling the pain from growing up amidst all of that dysfunction. He is cynical about marriage, yet desperately wants to marry and provide a secure home setting for his children. Yet he wonders if that is even possible. He questions his own ability to carry out a healthy relationship when he never saw one modeled in his own home.

There are a lot of Brents to be found among Generation X. Whether it is from growing up with addicted parents, being physically or sexually abused, or dealing with the divorce and remarriage of a parent, their family life has not been a very positive experience. As a result, they are full of doubt and resentment and wonder if the future will hold any hope for them.

Life Application and Implication For Ministry

1. If you are a parent, take an honest look at how you spend your time. How much do you spend in direct interaction with your children, giving them your undivided attention? Use this week for an experiment. Keep track of exactly how much time is spent each day with them. Watching TV together does not count (sorry). Before you do this, take a

guess at how much time you spend. Write that down. _____ hrs/minutes per day. How much did you actually spend? _____ Were you satisfied with what you found? If not, what can you do to change this situation?

2. Sit down with your children and teens and make a list of things that you would like to do together. Some things might take just a few minutes such as a quick Coke or cappuccino at the food court in the mall. Others might take a whole day, like a hike in the mountains, a fishing trip or taking in a professional ball game. Make two lists; one that has your choices and one that has theirs. Take the family calendar and alternate putting one choice from your lists on a week or month. Most importantly, enjoy your time together, whatever you choose to do.

3. What can the church do in the way of education and seminars to help build stronger marriages and families? I would encourage every congregation to sponsor a marriage enrichment retreat at least once a year. Perhaps the board or ministry team needs to sit down and look over the church calendar and consolidate some meetings and activities so that families are able to spend more time at home together rather than being further fragmented by obligations to the local congregation.

4. Does your church offer a divorce recovery group or a children of divorce support group? Pray about this need. What would it take to get one started in your community?

5. Blended families have some unique needs. They have custody and child sharing issues, holiday arrangements, and financial obligations to meet. What can the church do to help?

6. Michael Card said in *Servant* magazine, "Kids aren't just an inconvenience that you deal with. Kids are something that you give your life to." In what ways did parents and other adults communicate to Generation X that they were "inconvenient?" What can be done to remedy this situation? In what ways do you as a parent or youth worker communi-

cate with your life that kids are worth "giving your life to?"

7. Make a list of the members of your youth group. Then on a separate piece of paper make another list with the categories of: 1) Divorced Family, 2) Blended Family, 3) Unmarried Mother, 4) Intact But Dysfunctional Family; and 5) Intact and Healthy Family. Now place the members of the youth group underneath one of those categories. Where do most of your kids fall? What does this tell you about the needs of your kids and the direction your youth program needs to go? How can you begin implementing this program?

Notes

1. "Absentee Dads." *Current Thoughts & Trends*, 8 July 1992, 11.

2. Piper Lowell, "Out of Desperation," *Sojourners*, November 1994, 20.

3. Andres Tapia, "Reaching the First Post-Christian Generation," *Christianity Today*, 12 September 1994, 21.

4. Johann Goethe, "The Beginning (and the end) of Civilization," *Current Thoughts & Trends*, 11 February 1995, 18.

5. William Bennett, "Boys to Men," *Current Thoughts & Trends*, 11 June 1995, 18.

6. James C. Dobson and Gary L. Bauer, *Children At Risk: Winning the Battle for the Hearts and Minds of Your Children* (Dallas: Word Publishing, 1990), 155.

7. William Strauss & Neil Howe, *Generations*, 325.

8. "What Is So Unique About Generation X?" *Current Thoughts & Trends*, 11 June 1995, 30.

9. Geoffrey T. Holtz, *Welcome to the Jungle*, 27.

10. Strauss & Howe, *Generations*, 324.

11. Archibald D. Hart, *Children & Divorce: What to Expect: How to Help* (Waco: Word, 1982), 32.

12. Eugene C. Roehlkepartain (ed), "Teenage Attitudes About Divorce." *The Youth Ministry Resource Book* (Loveland: Group Books, 1988), 29.

13. George Barna, *The Future of the American Family* (Chicago: Moody Press, 1993), 88.

14. Barbara DaFoe Whitehead, "Dan Quayle Was Right" *The Atlantic Monthly*, April 1993, 62.

15. Barna, *Future of the American Family*, 86.

16. Whitehead, "Dan Quayle Was Right," 77.

17. Ibid.

18. Holtz, *Welcome to the Jungle*, 185.

19. "Facts About Families." *Current Thoughts & Trends*, 9 August 1993, 14.

20. Whitehead, "Dan Quayle Was Right," 71.

21. Holtz, *Welcome to the Jungle*, 37.

22. Deidre S. Laiken, *Daughters of Divorce: The Effects of Parental Divorce On Women's Lives* (New York: William Morrow, 1981), 161.

23. Whitehead, "Dan Quayle Was Right," 72.

24. Ibid.

25. For some excellent insights into the unique problems of blended family situations I would highly recommend: Laura Sherman Walters, *There's A New Family In My House!: Blending Stepfamilies Together* (Wheaton, IL: Harold Shaw Publishers, 1993); Tom & Adrienne Frydenger, *The Blended Family* (New York: Chosen Books, 1984) and Elizabeth Einstein, *The Stepfamily: Living, Loving & Learning* (Boston: Shambhala, 1985).

26. "Single Parents: Never-Marrieds Soon to Outnumber Divorced." *Current Thoughts & Trends*, 11 March 1995, 10.

27. "And Where's Dad?" *Current Thoughts & Trends*, 9 October 1993, 15.

28. Quoted in Whitehead, "Dan Quayle Was Right," 82.

29. Eugene C. Roehlkepartain (ed), "Spending Time With Parents." *The Youth Ministry Resource Book*, 32.

30. Merton Strommen and Irene Strommen, *The Five Cries of Parents* (San Francisco: Harper, 1985), 72.

31. Josh McDowell and Norm Wakefield, *The Dad Difference* (San Bernardino, CA: Here's Life, 1989), 13.

32. Not her real name, but the story is used with her permission.

33. Gary Dausey, *The Youth Leader's Sourcebook* (Grand Rapids: Zondervan, 1983), 17.

34. Warren S. Benson and Mark H. Senter III, eds., *The Complete Book of Youth Ministry* (Chicago: Moody Press, 1987), 83.

35. Christina Parker, *Children of Alcoholics: Growing Up Unheard* (Phoenix, AZ: Do It Now Foundation, 1986); quoted in Tom Klaus, *Healing Hidden Wounds: Ministering to Teenagers From Alcoholic Families* (Loveland, CO: Group Books, 1989) 19.

36. Vicky Lytle, "Children of Alcoholics: Recognizing Their 'Secret Suffering'" NEA Today, December 1987, 9; quoted in Tom Klaus, *Healing Hidden Wounds*, 19.

37. Lytle, "Children of Alcoholics," 9.

38. Charles Leerhsen, "Alcohol and the Family," *Newsweek*, 18 January 1988, 63.

39. Not his real name, but shared with permission.

Why Can't Gen X Read?

For the first time in the history of our country, the educational skills of one generation will not surpass, will not equal, will not even approach, those of their parents. — John Copperman in *A Nation at Risk: The Full Account*[1]

Given the yawning knowledge chasm — the gap between what they minimally should, and actually do, know (in matters historical, political and economic) — on what basis is the average teen voter to make his electoral selection: the candidate's hairstyle, taste in music, number of syllables in his last name? — Don Feder in the *Washington Times*[2]

Schools should be a place where children learn what they most want to know, instead of what we think they ought to know. — John Holt in *How Children Fail*[3]

The idea was no longer to "educate" the child in the traditional sense of filling him up with knowledge, but to free him from his dependence on teachers, schools, and books. — Diane Ravitch in *The Schools We Deserve*[4]

The dominant theme of the scant academic planning that did exist in the seventies and eighties was that the "self-esteem" of the student was as important — or even more so — than any particular academic goals. — Geoffrey T. Holtz in *Welcome to the Jungle: The Why Behind "Generation X"*[5]

Like many other people, I have long been appalled by the low quality and continuing deterioration of American education. . . . I am frankly surprised that the results are not even worse than they are. The incredibly counterproductive fads, fashions, and dogmas of American education — from kindergarten to the colleges — have yet to take their full toll, in part because all the standards of earlier times have not yet been completely eroded away. — Thomas Sowell in *Inside American Education*[6]

It should have been the best educational opportunity to come down the pike. Never had support or interest in education been higher. New facilities and the latest in technological equipment were made available to Generation X. People expected great things. What they got was a report that indicated this generation had scored the lowest on the Scholastic Aptitude Test (SAT), the American College Testing Program (ACT), as well as on the Iowa Test of Educational Development of any generation.[7] For the SAT, verbal skills had dropped thirty points in nine years and fifty-one points over a twenty year period. The average math scores fell from 502 in 1962-63 to 466 in 1980-81 — a drop of thirty-six points. In addition, the number of students scoring above 600 (generally considered an indication of academic excellence) declined 48%.

Gary Allen wrote in an article entitled "The Grave National Decline in Education":

> One poll reveals that only three percent of the nation's high-school seniors can correctly identify Alaska and Hawaii as the last two states admitted to the Union; . . . a minuscule four percent can name the three Presidents immediately preceding Gerald Ford; a quarter of those polled don't even realize that New Jersey is on the east coast and Oregon is on the west coast; and, fifty-six percent cannot identify the nation's most populous state.

> A "citizenship test" conducted with a grant from the Scherman Foundation revealed that only sixty percent of teenagers about to become eligible to vote could name the war in which states' rights was an issue; only fifty-seven percent knew Russia fought on our side in World War II; and, only fifty-five percent knew the nationality of Josef Stalin.

> In geography, ninety-three percent did manage to identify the capital of their own state. But only twenty-three percent had any idea of the distance between New York and San Francisco and a bare twenty-eight percent came anywhere near guessing the population of the United States. Forty-one percent did not know that Red China is the world's most populous nation, and sixty-one percent did not know that Mexico has more people than Canada.[8]

While the scores and abilities of Generation X were plummeting, their marks on their grade cards were going up overall. In 1966 teachers awarded 70% A's and B's and 30% C's to their students. In 1977 the amount of A's and B's rose to 80% and the percentage of C's given out fell to 20%.[9] When unsuspecting parents read their children's report cards, they honestly believed their children were doing well, in fact, excelling in their educational pursuits! What they failed to realize was that while their children's grades were rising, their knowledge was declining. The culprit was grade inflation. It reflected an educational philosophical shift which focused more on the student's "feelings" about himself, than on actual knowledge learned. Teachers became more concerned about their student's self-esteem than they did their ability to read, write and do math. Not wanting to hurt a student's self-esteem by giving them a low grade, teachers began giving high grades just as a matter of course, regardless of the quality or accuracy of the work. The result was devastating in the long run.

What Don't Our 17-Year-Olds Know?

- 31.9% do not know that Columbus discovered the New World before 1750.
- 40% are ignorant of the fact that the Japanese attack on Pearl Harbor occurred between 1939 and 1943.
- 75% could not place Lincoln's presidency within the correct twenty-year time span.
- 66% could not place the American Civil War in the fifty-year span between 1850 and 1900.
- 43% did not know that World War I occurred during the first half of the twentieth century.
- 50% could not place Franklin Roosevelt's presidency in the years between 1929 and 1946.

Source: *What Do Our 17-Year-Olds Know?*

According to Samuel Blumenfeld, America's "public schools are falling apart and academic standards are at their lowest. At least a million students emerge from high school each year as functional illiterates thanks to the educational malpractice rampant in American public schools."[10] A report in *Time* found that 13% of American seventeen-year-olds are functionally illiterate. That figure soars to 40% for minorities of the same age.[11] The

United States Department of Education estimates that our educational system has left us with 24 million functionally illiterate people. Only about 50% of our youth can read and comprehend a high school textbook. About 21% can read and comprehend college level materials. These are not people who never went to school, but for the most part, they are individuals who have spent eight to twelve years in public schools.

This gaping abyss in knowledge is not just a problem found in public schools. It is also a problem within the church. Today's teens don't know their Bible. Let me illustrate with an event that took place a little over ten years ago. I was the Dean of a High School week of church camp. Instead of following all of the traditional programming that had characterized this particular camp for so many years, I decided to introduce some creative alternatives to the camping program.

One evening during the scheduled social hour I had planned to divide the campers up into teams and play "Bible Family Feud," my variation on the then popular game show "Family Feud." The game was played by having the audience answer certain questions before the game began and the answers the contestants were seeking were based upon the audience response. The number one answer was the answer given by the most people. (It didn't matter if the answer was actually correct or not, just the fact that the majority of people gave it as an answer made it number one.)

A list of questions that I had prepared concerning general Bible knowledge was given to the campers to answer during registration. The next day the answers were compiled and arranged in descending order according to the number of campers who gave a particular response. The response given most frequently by the campers was the number one answer and so forth.

I was shocked and dismayed at the biblical ignorance displayed by these young people. For the most part these represented the cream of the crop from our churches. These were our best teens, the ones who had attended more Sunday

School and youth group meetings than any of their peers. But you would never know it from their answers. For example, I instructed them to name a king found in the Bible. Some answers I expected and was looking for were; "David," "Saul," "Solomon," "Nebuchadnezzar" and so forth. The number one answer given by the campers? *King James!* Get it? The King James Bible.

Another question I asked was, "Name one of the fruits of the Spirit found in Galatians 5:22-23." Once again, I expected to find "love, joy, peace, patience, etc." The number one answer? Survey says: "Apple."

This would be hilarious if it didn't signify such a serious problem. I am reminded of the prophecy found in Amos 8:11 "'The days are coming,' declares the Sovereign Lord, 'when I will send a famine through the land — not a famine of food or a thirst for water, but a famine of hearing the words of the Lord.'"

Sadly enough, my experience was not unique. Research has shown that biblical ignorance is now the norm, not the exception. A Gallup survey of America's Youth 1977-1988 found that 75% of teens surveyed believed in a personal God and 66% believed in life after death, but only 35% could name four or more of the Ten Commandments and only 3% could name all ten. Thirty-five percent of the teens could name the four gospels and 66% knew how many disciples Jesus had.[12]

The Why Behind the Fall

People want to know, "What went wrong?" "Is an entire generation just numb and dumb?" No, the fault lies with changing educational philosophies. These changes took place gradually over a period of time. Most people did not know what was happening until it was too late. The most widely quoted paragraph from the 1983 report from the National Commission on Excellence in Education, entitled "A Nation at Risk," summed up the plight well:

The educational foundations of our society are presently being eroded by a rising tide of mediocrity that threatens our very future as a nation and as a people. If an unfriendly foreign power had attempted to impose on America the mediocre educational performance that exists today, we might well have viewed it as an act of war. As it stands, we have allowed this to happen to ourselves.[13]

The cartoon character Pogo was prophetic, "I have found the enemy, and they are us." American education embraced the concepts of post-modern philosophy which proposed that there was no such thing as absolute truth. Everything was relative. This was carried over into the classroom. There was no body of knowledge or truths to be learned which would be considered essential for all people to know. Nor was it believed that there was any one set of values that was necessarily superior to any others that one should embrace and follow. The only thing that was left was opinion and personal preference. Values and truth were left up to the individual to discover for himself. Since it was all a matter of personal choice, one could not make a judgment about someone else's choice. What was right for you might not be right for someone else. What is truth for them might not be truth for you, but you must never judge someone else's opinion to be wrong. Tolerance and openness are the philosophical king and queen of the college curriculum. The belief that everything is relative is the one "truth" that is sacrosanct in today's liberal educational philosophy. Alan Bloom exposed this liberal agenda in his book, *The Closing of the American Mind*. He writes:

There is one thing a professor can be absolutely certain of: almost every student entering the university believes, or says he believes, that truth is relative. If this belief is put to the test, one can count on the students' reaction: they will be uncomprehending. That anyone should regard the proposition as not self-evident astonishes them, as though he were calling into question 2 + 2 = 4. . . . Relativism is necessary to openness; and this is the virtue, the only virtue, which all primary education for more than fifty years has dedicated itself to inculcating. [14]

Students were taught to believe that relativism was some-how inseparably linked to tolerance and an open mind. From their standpoint, the worst accusation that could be made about you was that you had a *closed* mind. Especially on a university campus where people were supposed to be open to new ideas, growth and insight. The problem is that they were so open minded that their brains fell out. They lost the ability to make any critical value judgments. If all things were relative and if relativism was inseparably linked to tolerance, then all that was left for them to do was to point out the different possibilities and choices without making any kind of judgment about the superiority of one choice over another. For to do so would indicate that one was intolerant and not open.

Incompetent Teachers

Not only did Generation X receive an inadequate philosophical educational base, but they suffered at the hands of incompetent teachers. For example, in 1983 the schoolteachers in Houston, Texas, were required to take a competency test. More than 60% of the teachers failed the reading part of the test. Forty-six percent failed the math section while 26% could not pass the writing exam. As if this weren't bad enough, 763 of the more than 3,000 teachers taking the test cheated! [15] In Louisiana only 53% of those applying for teaching jobs passed competency tests in 1978, and 63% in 1979. When asked about teacher applicants who failed, the director of certification for the state of Louisiana replied, "Obviously they're moving out of state to teach in states where the tests are not required." [16]

Time magazine did a cover story on the deplorable standards and quality of teachers in the public school system in America in its June 16, 1980 issue. A fifth grade teacher in Mobile, Alabama, the proud holder of a Master of Education degree from one of this nation's teacher's colleges, sends the following note home to one of her students' parents: "Scott is dropping in his studies [no punctuation] he acts as if he don't care. Scott want pass in his assignment at all, he a had a poem to learn and he fell to do it."[17] This is a precise copy of the note. With the dismal performance of this teacher and others like her in charge of educating Generation X, is it any wonder that their SAT and ACT scores plummeted?

How It All Played Out For Generation X

The Boomers of the '50s and '60s probably attended some of the finest schools in American history. They were excellent institutions because of the quality of the teachers who instructed the students. For the large part they were staffed by some of the brightest and most literate female members of the G.I. generation. Teaching was one of the few careers that was open to women at that time, and teachers received the respect and backing of the communities in which they worked. They held high personal standards and expected the same from their students.

For Generation X, that all changed. Advances in women's rights opened up other career fields which offered much more promising futures and better financial packages than teaching. The Vietnam war was the impetus for thousands of young men to enter college and prepare for a career in the teaching field in order to avoid the draft. They brought their anti-establishment agenda with them. All institutions were viewed with suspicion, including the traditional educational system. They set in motion a revolution. The purpose was to "free" America's children from all of the rules and restraints of the old authoritative system which "stifled" their creativity and innate desire to learn.

The predominant educational learning theories were influenced by Carl Rogers, a humanist psychologist who believed that mankind was basically good and that within each person was the power to reach one's potential. Rogers believed that one's potential was best reached when the individual was nurtured and encouraged to explore, learn and grow at his own pace and interest. Anyone who was pushed or encouraged to do an activity that was not self-initiated would develop feelings of resentment and conflict. A teacher's purpose was that of encouragement and support, but never direction or correction because the latter might hurt a child's esteem and desire to initiate and explore learning on his own. Education became "person-centered" and "experience-centered" rather than "fact-centered" or "skill-centered."

The very structure of new school buildings was designed to reflect an "open" atmosphere towards learning. Walls were torn down and several grades and classrooms were thrown into one large open area. Teachers and students competed with one another to be heard over the ensuing din. Open education became the fad which was foisted upon the unsuspecting youth of Generation X across America's cities.

> Open education was defined less in terms of what it was than in terms of what it was *not*: facts, subjects, rules, grades, bells, walls. Schools offered kids freedom to choose when and what to learn among various "learning tools" provided for them — often with no fixed schedule, sometimes without books, nearly always amid disruptive noise. . . . Existing curricula were suspect: Grammar was downplayed, basic readers were frowned upon, a "new math" de-emphasized the traditional ten's place, and civics lessons were taught with catchy jingles. Textbooks shifted their emphasis from accuracy and graduated difficulty to user "sensitivity" and "accessibility" — in others words, niceness and easiness.[18]

The whole emphasis in education became student oriented rather than fact or knowledge oriented. Teachers were more concerned about their pupil's self-esteem than their ability to read, write or do basic math. A book or an assignment was evaluated by the student in terms of how it made him feel, rather than looking for its universal message or truth.

Gen X students did a good job of learning what they had

been taught. In 1988 an international test was given to thirteen-year-olds. American students scored dead last among all of the nations who took the math test, but when asked to rate themselves on their ability to do math, American students ranked themselves first among all of the countries. In other words, they had great self-esteem, they *felt* like they were good at doing math — the only problem was that when push came to shove, they could not correctly solve the math problems presented on the test. In contrast, only 23% of the Korean children who took the test rated themselves as good at solving math problems, but as a group they scored the highest of all the nations. The emphasis in American education on developing positive self-esteem seems to be a success, but at what price?

The end result of this emphasis upon "feeling good" rather than upon performance was simply that students did not learn. They did not learn the fundamental skills needed to compete and perform in a satisfactory manner in today's job market. A good number of Xers cannot even read a simple operator's manual or compose a grammatically correct and comprehensible memo. Because of their lack of skills, the only work they are qualified for is some type of McJob in the food service industry at minimum wage, long hours with no benefits.

Generation X was deceived. They were deceived by the very people they trusted the most — their parents, their teachers and their community. From the time they entered grade school and all the way up through high school they had been told that there were no standards, no minimum performance levels that everyone had to attain. All they had to do was be in touch with their feelings and just let their feelings be their guide. There was nothing to worry about, after all, they had all received passing grades from their teachers.

It usually wasn't until after graduation that the light began to dawn upon them. When they went to apply for admission to the college of their choice or attempt to secure a good paying job, they found that there had indeed been standards and that they had failed to meet them. Not only had they failed to meet them, but no one much cared now how they felt about that failure.

Sadly, the present situation has not changed much. Over one-third of 15-17 year-olds (35%) have either dropped out of school or are enrolled below their appropriate grade level, up from 29% in 1980. Most high school seniors (71%) spend only one hour or less on homework each night, and 56% read ten or fewer pages per day. Adding and subtracting two-digit numbers is a skill 25% of nine-year-olds have yet to master.[19]

Life Application and Implication For Ministry

1. It has been said that those who choose to ignore the events of history are doomed to repeat them. What implications does this have for Generation X when they as a group have scored so poorly on historical knowledge?
2. Is your Sunday School and youth group curriculum more "feeling" or "fact" oriented? Why? What does it need to be?
3. Since a large number of teens have been deemed "functionally illiterate," it is likely that you will have a number in your church and youth group who cannot read. What ramifications does that have for the Sunday School and youth group programs and curriculum? Brainstorm alternative ways to present the gospel message that does not require a great deal of reading skills.
4. Write up and administer your own poll on basic Bible facts and present the findings in your own version of "Bible Family Feud" for youth group of youth night.
5. Does your church/Sunday School/youth group use: (Check those that apply)
   _____ videos _____ audio tapes _____ drama _____ role play _____ slides _____ dramatic reading _____ music
6. What other creative ways can you come up with that would be an effective means of presenting the gospel to a generation of kids who do not like nor have the ability to read?

Notes

1. The National Commission on Excellence in Education, *A Nation at Risk: The Full Account* (Cambridge, MA: U.S.A. Research, 1984), 13.

2. Don Feder in the *Washington Times*, quoted in Neil Howe and Bill Strauss, *13th Gen*, 26.

3. John Holt, *How Children Fail* (New York: Delacorte, 1964), 289.

4. Diane Ravitch, *The Schools We Deserve* (New York: Basic Books, 1985), 86.

5. Geoffrey T. Holtz, *Welcome to the Jungle*, 112.

6. Thomas Sowell, *Inside American Education: The Decline, The Deception, The Dogmas* (New York: The Free Press, 1993), ix.

7. Ernest L. Boyer, *High School: A Report on Secondary Education in America* (New York: Harper & Row, 1983) 23,25,32.

8. Gary Allen, "The Grave National Decline in Education," *American Opinion*, 22 March 1979, 1,2,4.

9. Tim LaHaye, *The Battle for the Public Schools: Humanism's Threat to our Children* (Old Tappan, NJ: Fleming H. Revell Company, 1983), 25.

10. Samuel L. Blumenfeld, *NEA: Trojan Horse in American Education* (Boise, ID: The Paradigm Co., 1984), xii.

11. *Time*, 14 August 1989.

12. Robert Bezilla, ed., *America's Youth 1977-1988* (Princeton, NJ: The Gallup Organization, 1988), 141.

13. Quoted in Ronald H. Nash, *The Closing of the American Heart: What's Really Wrong With America's Schools* (Probe Books, 1990), 19.

14. Allan Bloom, *The Closing of the American Mind* (New York: Simon & Schuster, 1987), 25-26.

15. Blumenfeld, *NEA*, 211.

16. "Help, Teacher Can't Teach," *Time*, 16 June 1980, 55.

17. Ibid.

18. Howe & Strauss, *13th Gen*, 73.

19. "Educational Malaise." *Current Thoughts & Trends,* 9 February 1993, 25.

Just Do It!
The Values and Beliefs of Generation X

But then I must remind myself we are living creatures — we have religious impulses — we must — and yet into what cracks do these impulses flow in a world without religion? It is something I think about every day. Sometimes I think it is the only thing I should be thinking about. — Douglas Coupland in *Life After God*[1]

. . . What is the most meaningful aspect of your life? People of older generations tended to answer "family" without hesitation. Among Generation X and those younger, answers ranged from "lunch" to "nothing." When they were pressed, though, their overwhelming response was "friends." — William Mahedy & Janet Bernardi in *A Generation Alone: Xers Making a Place in the World*[2]

To the typical Buster, there is no such thing as absolute truth. Statistically, 70% claim that absolute truth does not exist, that all truth is relative and personal. This view is supported by their belief that everything in life is negotiable. — George Barna in *Baby Busters: The Disillusioned Generation*[3]

Many of them are moved to having sex not by the love or compassion or other urges that make sense to adults, but by a craving for intimacy that has gone unfulfilled by their families. — Geoffrey T. Holtz in *Welcome to the Jungle: The Why Behind "Generation X"*[4]

She sees herself as post-ideological, in some ways even post-religious. She's hesitant to impose her beliefs (on everything from school prayer to abortion) on others. — Neil Howe and Bill Strauss in *13th Gen: Abort, Retry, Ignore, Fail?*[5]

Generation X got their not-so-flattering name because it was believed by Boomers and other older members of previous generations that they did not believe in anything, stand for anything or do anything. They were tagged the "do-nothing" generation. They were looked upon as apathetic and not as altruistic or idealistic as previous generations.

The truth of the matter is that the members of Generation X are just as altruistic and involved in causes as any previous generation. The difference is that Generation X doesn't get any credit for their involvement and commitment because they do it differently from previous generations. The Boomers, the generation preceding them, loved to be involved in causes. They did it as a group. They gathered in parks and university campuses and sang songs, listened to speeches and protested.

Xers scorn this model. They don't care much for speeches or rhetoric. They want to see action. Rather than talking about it, Xers "just do it." They cynically view their elders and previous generations as "talking the talk," but not "walking the walk." Xers are just as likely to be involved in a cause as previous generations, but they choose to do it without all of the fanfare and hoopla that surrounded their Boomer parents in the sixties. Boomers got involved in causes en masse, they protested in groups. Members of Generation X are more likely to be involved on an individual basis. A typical Xer might spend some time on the weekend picking up trash along a river helping to clean up the environment or volunteering at a local nursing home. Xers believe in helping to make the world a better place, but their solution involves doing it one person at a time instead of in large groups with the media covering the event hoping to get a spot on the 6 o'clock news. "Xers are no less interested in the world's global needs, nor are they less altruistic, but, as always, they are much quieter about what they are doing."[6]

> Nearly half volunteer their time to help needy people in their area. Critically important, though, is the realization that much of the volunteerism happens apart from organization-driven efforts; that is, Busters will lend a hand to the needy on their own, or in conjunction with friends and family who share the desire to make a difference. Also note that Busters are much more likely to engage in volunteer activity that aids domestic causes than that aimed at minimizing international problems.[7]

Xers are a generation of pragmatists. They don't care much for philosophical debate or clever theories. They just want to know what works. The motto for this generation is found on their sneakers — "Just Do It!"

Xer Involvement

- More young people volunteer than at any time in the past 30 years.
- When asked whether each of us has an obligation to make a contribution to our community, over 70% of 16- to 29-year-olds said "yes," the highest percentage of any generation.
- Almost 45% of all college students surveyed said that influencing social values was an essential or very important goal in life. This represents an all-time high in the past 25 years.
- One in three consider becoming a community leader a very important or essential goal—more than double the number who thought so when the question was first asked in 1972.
- Almost half of all 18- to 24-year-olds volunteer at least one day a year, and about 25% of all college undergrads volunteer an average of five hours a week for a community service program.
- 40% of all first-year college students participated in some form of organized demonstration during 1992—more than double the number that did so in 1966 and 1967, during the Vietnam War and civil rights uprisings.

Source: *Revolution X: A Survival Guide for Our Generation*

The way Generation X communicates with one another is a reflection of their life philosophy. It is very blunt and functional. They have not produced the poets and speech writers like the children of the sixties did. Their communication is a very "bottom line," "results-oriented" style. "We are not interested in language for language's sake, but in what language accomplishes in helping us survive."[8]

Exit Absolute Truth

One of the reasons that Generation X approaches life so pragmatically is because they have lost their moral base. Decisions are not made based upon what is right or wrong, but simply what works. The explanation for this is simply that Generation X does not believe that there is a universal set of ethical values or truths for all people for all time. For them everything is relative. It is simply a matter of the situation and personal opinion. Over 70% of Generation X believe there is no such thing as absolute truth. (An absolute truth is one that is true for all people in all societies, in every time period and in every situation.) Rejecting the idea of absolute truth, Xers believe that everything in life is negotiable. "In this way of viewing the world, since there are no absolutes, all decisions and realities can be debated until an accommodation is reached between the parties involved."[9]

Teen Attitudes			
Statement	Agree	Disagree	Don't Know
What is right for one person in a given situation might not be right for another person in a similar situation.	91%	8%	1%
When it comes to matters of morals and ethics, truth means different things to different people; no one can be absolutely positive that they know the truth.	80%	19%	1%
There is no such thing as "absolute truth"; two people could define "truth" in conflicting ways and both could still be correct.	72%	28%	< 0.5 %
Lying is sometimes necessary	57%	42%	1%
Source: George Barna, *Generation Next*			

One very serious and negative result of this lack of absolutes is the rising crime rate among the young. Rowland Nethaway summed up the problem this way:

> Adults have always complained about their youth, but this is different. There have always been wild and rebellious kids who would go off the track and do something wrong. But they knew where the track was and what was wrong. Many of today's youth don't seem to know right from wrong. Children are robbing, maiming and killing on whims, and with no pity and no remorse.[10]

While members of Generation X who claim to be Christians might say that they *do* believe in absolutes, contrary to their non-Christian peers, nonetheless, the evidence is in and it shows that they are living out their lives *just as if* there were no absolutes. The Barna Research group compiled information from 3,795 youth from thirteen denominations throughout the U.S. and Canada. The majority of the kids involved in this survey indicated that they had made a personal commitment to Jesus Christ, and yet the survey revealed that an alarming number were involved in inappropriate, immoral and even illegal behavior. The survey showed that in the past three months alone:

- Two out of every three (66%) church kids (ages 11-18) lied to a parent, teacher or other adult.
- Six in ten (59%) lied to their peers.
- One in three (36%) cheated on an exam.
- Nearly one in four (23%) smoked a cigarette or used another tobacco product.
- One in nine (12%) had gotten drunk.
- Nearly one in ten (8%) has used illegal, non-prescription drugs.

Source: Barna, *Baby Busters*

Smorgasbord Spirituality

The lack of absolutes in the worldview of Generation X affects all other aspects of their lives, from religion to politics to sex. Generation X is very interested in spiritual things, but do not make the mistake of assuming that "spiritual" is to be equated with "Christian" for the typical Xer. Because their worldview holds no absolute truths, this carries over into their spiritual realm. For the typical Xer, no one religious denomination or religious belief is the only *right* one for all people at all times. It is more a matter of "what works for you." Since they have rejected the concept of absolute truth, there can be no objective standard by which to measure any one belief. Judgment, then, is based upon feelings, experience and practicality. If a particular church or religious organization provided a spiritual experience in which an Xer felt inspired, helped or gained some practical insight, he would deem that church or religious organization as one that had proven itself to be true because he "felt helped" by it. If it provided him with something that he needed, something that helped him survive, then it was true for him. The mere fact that it worked would give it validity in the eyes of an Xer because of his pragmatic base.

For the most part, Xers are wary of all organized religion. It is their parents' religion and those who control the "power" in society; the very same people who neglected and abused them. It is part of the system and they don't trust the system.

Christians, especially fundamentalists, are difficult for Xers to accept because of their exclusive doctrinal claims. Christians believe that Jesus Christ is the *only* way to heaven, the *only* religion that offers true salvation, and the *only* source of spiritual truth. The relativism and tolerance of Generation X finds that unacceptable. They see all religions as having equal authority and validity and anyone who claims to have exclusive insight to spiritual truth or God is intolerant. For the Xer, no one person has the right to make a judgment concerning another's spiritual experience or their methodology at arriving at spiritual truth.

> "I'm not religious or antireligious," said one Xer I talked to. "Maybe there is a God. I sure wouldn't rule out the possibility. But I don't rule it in, either. I mean, how does anybody really know? How can anybody say that Christians are right and Moslems are wrong? To criticize or condemn other religions, to say that some people are going to go to hell because they call their god 'Allah' instead of 'Jesus' — I mean, that just seems totally ridiculous to me."[11]

Xers are not as cognitive oriented as they are affective oriented. By that, I mean that they don't concern themselves as much with ideas and arguments as they do with experiences and feelings. To them, God is basically a concept — a nontangible idea.

> While we accept the idea that God exists (at least superficially), we don't spend much time thinking deeply about God. We don't so much reject religious faith as neglect it. We have more important and more tangible things to think about. If we can't see, hear, touch, or taste it, it doesn't have an impact on our lives.[12]

I will never forget when this neglect of God concerning Generation X was made real to me. I had just attended a week of seminars and main sessions at the National Youth Leader's Convention held on the campus of Ozark Christian College. Dave Busby was one of the main speakers. He told of his passion to correct teens' misconceptions about God. In his travels across the country speaking to crowds of young people, he had discovered four basic misconceptions that young people had about God. Dave would ask them, "If you could sit down with God, knee to knee, toe to toe, how would God react to you? Dave found that they either saw God as 1) distant from them; 2) disappointed in them; 3) disgusted with them or 4) angry at them.

I thought this insight was powerful and I decided to develop a sermon around correcting those four misconceptions. I recruited my good friend and fellow professor at Ozark Christian College, Mark Moore, to do a sermon in dialogue with me. The plan was that Mark would voice the misconceptions of the teens and I would share the corrected insights about God.

I was excited about this sermon as we were developing it. Looking for feedback and insight, I shared the four misconceptions about God with my middle son, Aaron, who was a Junior in high school at that time. I asked him to identify which misconception about God was most common amongst his friends and school mates. After a lot of thought and struggling to find an answer, he said, "Dad, none of them. God's not even an issue for most of the guys at school. They don't even give the question of God a second thought. It's just not a part of their lives." Their lives were spent in search of the next exciting experience, not in deep consideration of some theological concept.

Because of their pragmatism and lack of absolutes, if an Xer did feel a need for a religious commitment, he would most likely not commit to any orthodox view of Christianity, but develop a religious belief of his own; a sort of spiritual smorgasbord. He might borrow something from Christianity, something from Islam, a little something from Native American religion, a dash of new age philosophy blended in with a touch of Eastern mysticism and meditation, and, voila — instant personalized religion. As long as it worked for him, that was all the proof he needed that it was valid.

According to a study by George Barna, only six out of ten teenagers take an orthodox Christian view of God, defining Him as "the all-powerful, all-knowing, perfect creator of the universe who rules the world today." That leaves four out of ten teens who hold to a different view of God. One in five hold to a "new age" outlook where either everyone is God or God is just some impersonal force. Some believe there are many different gods and one in five don't know what God means or how to define God.[13]

There is alarming evidence that even Christian teens who claim to be "born again" do not live out their lives in accordance to the absolute standards of the Bible, but reflect virtually the same amount of involvement in undesirable behaviors as those teens who did not identify themselves as "born again." About the only major difference that was found between the two groups was in "religious" categories.[14]

Generation X is spiritual — it is just not very Christian in the orthodox sense. Nine out of ten teens would still identify themselves as "Christian,"[15] however, you must understand that when they use the term "Christian" they are only using it in some generic sense. They would equate all Americans as Christians by default. After all, what else would you be? Since this is our nation's heritage, as opposed to Buddhist or Muslim, they would say that they were Christians by national heritage, but not Christians in the moral or spiritual sense in the way that the church understands the term.

BEHAVIORAL DIFFERENCES BETWEEN CHRISTIAN AND NON-CHRISTIAN TEENS		
	Born Again?	
Perspective	Yes	No
Discussed your religious views with other kids your age	79%	56%
Have ever felt like you were experiencing God's presence	64%	33%
Volunteered your time to help needy people	49%	44%
Have ever watched an X-rated or pornographic movie	32%	41%
Have cheated on a test, exam or other evaluation	29%	27%
Have had sexual intercourse	23%	29%
Have stolen money or some other material thing	6%	7%
Have looked through a pornographic magazine	5%	8%
Have used an illegal, non-prescriptive drug	4%	11%
Have tried to commit suicide	3%	7%
Source: George Barna, *Generation Next*		

Xers prefer a do-it-yourself kind of spirituality which is heavy in the experiential. A typical Xer has little time for talking theology concerning the hereafter. He would rather pour his energy into some physical experience that stretched him in the here and now. Rock climbing, sail-boarding, surfing or cycling might be considered a "spiritual experience" for an Xer. "Taking risks, playing hard, going to extremes — this is how many Xers define spirituality."[16]

The Politics of Generation X

Rob Nelson and Jon Cowan, two Xers, were concerned about the apathy and lack of political involvement they saw amongst the members of their generation so they formed a political action group entitled "Lead. . . Or Leave." They traveled around the country and organized rallies in dozens of cities on hundreds of college and high school campuses with the goal of organizing the voting members of the twentysomething generation. It was a political and social call to action.

But they were greeted with a less than enthusiastic reception from the members of their own generation. They found very few members of the X Generation who really believed that their individual involvement and contributions would make much of a difference with the huge national problems facing the country. Xers look at the most serious national problems such as homelessness, AIDS and the national debt as too large and complex for them to understand, much less fix. It should come as no surprise. This was the ". . .generation that was raised on images of politics and government gone sour: Vietnam, Watergate, the $500 billion S & L scandal, and Iran-Contra."[17]

While Xers may not be very involved in politics or put much faith in the political process, that does not mean they are void of political concerns. They are very much concerned about education, the environment and the out of sight national debt, especially the Social Security system and welfare program which has placed an inordinate amount of responsibility on Generation X to maintain. "Our Social Security system is so insecure that it will ultimately require a 40% tax hike on future generations to remain solvent."[18] Generation X pays the highest relative taxes of any age group in America, and yet they receive the fewest direct benefits.

When Xers do get involved in the political process, they are neither liberal nor conservative. They do not hold to traditional party loyalties, but vote according to issue. Overall they do tend to vote on the conservative side, especially when it comes to economics and finances. They want to see a balanced budget. They feel resentful about the huge national debt that has accumulated as a result of the spending policies of previous generations. Already the national debt is large enough to pay Michael Jordan's salary for over one and a half million years. "Even if Washington makes a determined effort to stop borrowing more money, our generation will inherit, by the turn of the millennium, a $6 trillion debt — more than 20 times what it was when the first members of our generation were born in 1960."[19] They don't like the fact that they have been left holding the bag for the financial irresponsibility of previous generations.

While they usually vote conservative on economic issues, they vote liberal on many personal issues, such as choice. An

Xer might be personally opposed to abortion, but will vote pro-choice because of his or her commitment to tolerance and the belief that every person has the right to decide what is right for his own life and that no outside person or institution should take that right away from him.

Gay rights is another area where Xers tend to vote liberally. A slight majority of Xers (55%) personally believe that gay sex is immoral, but because of their prevailing worldview, that there are no absolutes, they believe that people should be allowed to do whatever they want as long as it does not harm others. Forty-four percent believe that gay couples should be allowed to get married and 38% believe that they should also be allowed to adopt and raise children.[20]

Xers tend to flop-flop back and forth. They are comfortable with change and will vote for change. In the early '80s the choice of young voters changed from that of Democratic support (10 point advantage) to an 18 point advantage in favor of the Republican party (52 to 34%).[21] This was a significant change because it made Xers the first pro-Republican young Americans since the 1920s. In fifteen out of sixteen polls taken between 1981 and 1988, Xers gave Ronald Reagan a higher approval rating than did any older age bracket. They liked Reagan because he represented stability. Xers had enough chaos in their own personal lives; they didn't need society to add any more chaos to their overstressed systems. Reagan represented a return to normalcy after all of the social and political upheaval of the sixties. Xers needed and wanted his calm assurance and strong, confident leadership.

But even though they were fiercely loyal to Reagan, that did not make them fiercely loyal to the Republican party. Married Xers did vote for George Bush in the 1992 election by a margin of 2-to-1. However, single Xers swung their support to Bill Clinton at a rate of 3-to-1. He was the candidate who stood for "change" and Xers like change. Besides, he seemed to be the only candidate who made an effort to enter into their world and to hear them out. Remember his playing the sax on TV? He may not be an accomplished musician, but he pulled off a powerful political move with that performance because he looked "cool" to Generation X, and, remember, for an Xer "Image is everything."

> My generation is so inundated with information that we don't know what truth is anymore. We suffer from information overload. We see the political ads on TV and we are confused. We will vote for the one who projects the most trustworthy or caring image, or the one with whom we most identify. We vote out of feelings, not convictions. We don't know who's lying and who's telling the truth. So we vote for the one with the most attractive image.
>
> Issues are complex. Image is simple. Thirteeners like it simple.[22]

The politics of Xers is based on pragmatism, not ideology. They shun the global political interests of previous generations and prefer to see their politics carried out on the local level. They have watched older Americans talk endlessly about global problems such as hunger, racism, poverty and war — but with very little success at changing or curing any of those ills. Xers want something they can personally get involved in and see some concrete results from their efforts. They are more likely to push for recycling programs in their city and on their college campuses than to demonstrate for world peace.

The Sex Generation

As you might expect, a generation that has been raised to believe that there are no moral absolutes is a generation that is sexually active and they are becoming sexually active at an earlier age. Consider the following from Josh McDowell's *Why Wait?*

✠ 50% of today's sexually active nineteen-year-old males had their first sexual experience between the ages of eleven and thirteen.

✠ Most research shows that the average age for first having sex is fifteen for girls and fourteen for boys.

✠ Among the middle school boys who admit to sexual activity, the average age at loss of virginity was 11.1; for the sexually active girls, 11.7.

✠ According to the sexually active high school boys, the average age at which they lost their virginity was 13.2; average age for girls was 14.6.

✠ Each year, 30,000 of the girls who become pregnant are under fourteen years of age.[23]

While these figures might not represent the average experience of *most* teens, they do represent a significant number of teens; enough for considerable concern. The current trend continues to see sexual involvement at an earlier age. Generation X has to deal with peer pressure, media pressures, marketing pressures, cultural pressures and biological pressures for sexual involvement at a time when they are not emotionally or cognitively able to handle all the ramifications of such an important decision. The consequences of involvement are now much more serious for the Xer than for those in earlier generations. The World War II generation associated sex with procreation and marriage. The Baby Boom generation associated sex with free love. Generation X has been forced to associate sex with death because of the AIDS epidemic. Kim Blum of Redlands College summed it up well when he said, "The sexual revolution is over and everybody lost."[24]

Even though the specter of AIDS hovers over the Xer, he is still unlikely to change his attitudes about what constitutes proper and improper sexual behavior. When asked if schools should teach abstinence or encourage condom use, Xers overwhelmingly voted on the side of condom use. Only 19% of Xers voted for abstinence while 60% voted for condom use. When asked the same question 39% of Boomers voted for abstinence with 51% in support of condoms. The Silent or Builder generation (the grandparents of Xers) showed the greatest difference in values by a majority vote of 58% in favor of teaching abstinence with only 30% in favor of encouraging the use of condoms.[25]

Twenty percent of Xers who are currently single have had sexual intercourse with a married person and more than 75% of single Xers have engaged in sexual intercourse with another single. Only 23% of single Xers claim to be virgins.[26] "The stigma of premarital sex has all but disappeared, having been transferred to virginity."[27]

One might ask, "With the potential of AIDS hanging over every illicit sexual encounter, why do Xers still insist on engaging in such behavior?" What motivates them to go against what they know is the safest and best choice for their lives? The answer has nothing to do with sex per se, but everything to do with the need for affection and love.

I remember reading in the newspaper about a situation that took place in San Antonio, Texas. The local Health Department was alarmed because a number of young girls between the ages of 12 and 16 had requested AIDS tests. It was discovered that they had submitted to an initiation rite into a gang. The initiation involved having unprotected sex, at least once, with a member of the gang who had already been identified as HIV positive.

When I first read this I was dumbfounded! I have seen people who have died a slow, horrible death because of AIDS. Who in their right mind would knowingly submit to such a thing? Then I realized, it wasn't a matter of the mind at all. It was a matter of the heart.

Kids don't join gangs because they have a desire to steal car stereos, do drugs or participate in drive-by shootings. Kids join gangs because they are looking for a substitute family. A gang is the family they never had. Gang members are fiercely loyal to each other and will do anything for one another, even risk their lives if necessary. Gang members are committed to each other. The girls in San Antonio were willing to risk their lives so that they might be accepted into that substitute "family" and have the emptiness in their lives filled. If families were doing a better job of fulfilling their God-given responsibilities, fewer teens would have to seek out substitute love and affection through illicit sex. "Promiscuity, STDs and teen pregnancies may be less a result of the sexual revolution than a symptom of a malnourished home life."[28]

As you might expect, a generation with no moral absolutes is also going to be more tolerant of homosexual behavior. Only 3% of Barna's research among Generation X admitted to have participated in gay sex, and they indicated that homosexual behavior was wrong by a slight majority (55%). But that still leaves a sizable amount who are tolerant, if not outright in favor of it. As noted previously, 44% indicated they were in favor of changing laws so that homosexual couples could get married and 38% also believed that homosexual couples should be allowed to adopt and raise children.[29]

Their "tolerance" for sexual expression at any time in any way with anybody has found its limits, however. There has been a backlash in regard to their lack of moral absolutes concerning what constitutes acceptable sexual behavior between two people. This was first voiced by certain feminist groups who raised the country's awareness concerning the growing problem of date rape and gang rape on many college campuses and universities. Athletic dorms and frat houses were especially singled out as places where young women were routinely being taken advantage of sexually against their wills at certain parties. The solution that has been implemented by a number of colleges is to approve a politically correct guide to dating and sexual behavior. Antioch College in Ohio has gone so far as to create a school policy which requires students who are dating to obtain written permission before engaging in any behavior which might be considered sexual. They must obtain written permission for each advanced stage of intimacy. Anyone who violates or refuses to cooperate with this program is expelled from school.

Concerns of Gen X Teens

The concerns of the teens belonging to Generation X reflect their pragmatic worldview. They are not as likely to be concerned about global issues as much as they are about issues which immediately affect them and their survival. For the most part they have not involved themselves in politics and world causes like their Boomer parents because they see politics are a part of the system and the system has let them down. The worldwide political concerns that their parents involved themselves with still remain as problems today. We have not seen an end to world hunger, poverty, racism or war so they see this type of involvement as futile. It needs to be local. It needs to be personal. It needs to be immediate, not off somewhere in the uncertain future.

So what are the major issues concerning teenagers today? Barna found that the top five issues were: 1) Education-related concerns (45%); 2) Relationships (24%); 3) Emotional pressure (17%); 4) Physical threats, violence (13%); and 5) Financial difficulties.[30]

Why is education the number one concern for Xers when they have consistently performed poorly on the ACT, SAT and other college readiness exams? Because they know that if they are going to have even the remotest chance of obtaining a decent paying job in today's society, the minimum requirement for entry level in that job market is a college degree. Since moving to an information and service oriented society, the number of good paying factory and industrial jobs which do not require a high degree of educational skills have become almost nonexistent. Xers see their only alternatives as making the grade and getting a college degree or learning how to say, "Would you like fries with your hamburger?" They don't want to end up working long hours at some low-paying, dead end McJob. Education is their best bet. Unfortunately, it is one for which they have been poorly prepared. It frightens and angers them to know that theirs will be the first generation in the

United States to have a lower standard of living than their parents.

Because of their poor educational abilities and skills, they feel betrayed by the very people who were responsible for their life preparation. Now they are angry and resentful. One of the reasons that Generation X seems so indifferent and lackadaisical about societal concerns is because they choose *not* to be involved. It is their way of saying "In your face!" "As a culture you let us down, so we reject your culture."

Relational issues score high on their list of concerns because friends have taken the place of the absent family. They need someone to fill in the void left by absentee parents who will love them as they are and share their concerns and dreams. Friends help them decide major issues in their lives and help to lighten the load of emotional stress by their reassuring presence.

Generation X is plagued by stress. The number of teens who feel stressed out over life has increased from 25% in 1990 to nearly 40% today.[31] Increasing numbers of teens are hospitalized each year because of stress-related disorders. There is a significant amount of stress that comes from simply dealing with the normal developmental issues that all teens go through, but it is aggravated by the lack of parental guidance. David Elkind, in his classic book, *All Grown Up and No Place to Go*, chronicles the many struggles that teens go through because of the withdrawal of parental guidance and the lack of societal passages. Teens are stressed out over school and grades, sexual choices and peer pressure. Financial concerns cloud their future.

Bill Mahedy is a former teacher, missionary and army chaplain. For the past twelve years he has been a college chaplain and young adult pastor for the Episcopal Church in San Diego. He has spent a great deal of time ministering to college students from the '60s through the '90s. He has documented a disturbing trend.[32] The college students he works with today remind him of the Vietnam veterans that he worked with after the war who suffered from posttraumatic stress disorder (PTSD).

PTSD is the result of experiencing too many intensely emotional situations, especially ones where you perceive your life as being in danger. Because survival is the chief goal, the intense and powerful emotions of the crisis situation are often buried in order to take care of the business at hand. These intense, repressed emotions will resurface later in one form or another causing serious trouble and distress. Nightmares, flashbacks, sleep disorders, violent behavior, depression, and an inability to relate on a deep emotional level are all common symptoms of PTSD.

Countless numbers of young people from Generation X were physically and sexually abused as children. Others were psychologically abused through neglect or the result of growing up in a dysfunctional family. An increasing number of young people growing up in our large cities are exposed to gang violence and random drive-by shootings. For many adolescents who are a part of this next generation, life has been a war zone in every sense of the word. The chief goal of those growing up in these conditions? Survival. We should not be surprised when they exhibit the same symptoms as war veterans. Many are veterans. It is just that we haven't recognized their battle zone.

Generation X and the Work Place

One of the main criticisms of Generation X by Boomers especially is that they have no drive or ambition when it comes to jobs. Boomers have been characterized as selling their souls to the corporation. They are willing to work long hours, neglect their families and do whatever it takes just to get ahead.

Xers despise those values. They despise them because they are the primary victims of that particular marketplace ethic. Xers went home to an empty house and learned how to entertain themselves with the TV and video games while their absent parents worked overtime trying to inch their way up the corporate ladder. Because of this, Generation X will only work the minimum amount of hours needed to make ends meet. Boomers see a career as an end in itself. Xers see a job as a necessary evil. They work only to have enough money to pay their bills and to enable them to spend time in some activity of their choice with their friends.

Xers also have very little interest in being "part of the team" in some large corporation. They are highly individualistic. Corporations are institutions and they believe that institutions can't be trusted. Xers rely on the one thing that they have had to rely on to get them through growing up, and that is themselves. They know no loyalties except to themselves and their friends.

This does not mean that Generation X is unwilling to work. Quite the opposite. In fact, the proportion of teenagers who held part-time jobs was 50% higher in 1980 than it was in 1960. About two-thirds to three-fourths of high school age teenagers were employed during the 1980s. A 1981 survey titled "High School and Beyond" found that the average high school sophomore boy worked 15 hours each week and the average girl 10.5 hours. By their senior year, both boys and girls added about another six or seven hours to their work schedule. Besides going to school, the average employed senior was working the equivalent of an adult part-time job. About one student in ten worked 35 hours or more each week which is the equivalent of a full-time job.

At first this seems good. It stirs the soul of most adults to know that young people are out there "learning the value of a dollar." But there were some very negative affects of this. The first casualty of high youth employment was school. Students' grades suffered because many did not have time to finish their homework or study for tests. Others worked such late hours that they would fall asleep in class. Students who began working long hours at an earlier age were also more likely to be at risk for dropping out of school.

School extracurricular activities also suffered. With a large proportion of the student body working, there were less students who could make a commitment to sports, drama, band and other after school clubs and activities. Church youth groups also saw attendance fall at regularly scheduled meetings and activities because of teens' prior commitment to a job schedule.

The second serious consequence of teens holding part-time jobs was that most of them did not have any kind of financial accounting for how they spent their money. Very few teens who worked did so out of necessity to contribute to the families' overall income. They were not working to build character or save for college. They simply wanted more spending money. In 1986 American teenagers made 49.8 *billion* dollars collectively at their part-time jobs.[33] One-third of that total figure they spent on clothes and jewelry. The rest was spent on entertainment (fast food, movies, tapes and CD's) and electronic equipment.

This extra spending money caused many of the members of Generation X to develop extravagant tastes and to become comfortable with having a lot of discretionary money to spend at will. They were not paying any rent or helping with the family bills so it was all theirs to spend any way they wanted. The cost of a particular item was not really a concern for them, and they became accustomed to having quality things.

The problem comes when they want to leave home and set out on their own. The minimum wage jobs that satisfied their needs in high school while living at home could not provide the same standard of living once they left home and had to pay rent, utilities, car payments, food, etc. Not only could these minimum wage jobs not provide them with the standard of living to which they had been accustomed, but there was a scarcity of jobs available which could. "A 1992 MTV survey of one thousand young adults aged eighteen to twenty-nine found that they considered a lack of jobs or economic opportunity to be the single greatest obstacle facing their generation, with two thirds believing this."[34] Xers' response to this lack of jobs and opportunity has been one of frustration and anger. Searching for a solution to their money problems, some have moved back home (thus the origin of the term "Boomerang" kids to describe this generation) to be able to stretch their income dollar, but moving back home has its own unique set of problems.

Not only are Xers faced with working minimum wage jobs, but minimum wage has 26% less purchasing power today than it did in 1970.[35] Add to this the fact that Social Security takes a much larger bite out of the Xer's check than it did his parents or grandparents. From 1937 to 1950, the Social Security tax, employer and employee combined was only 2% of a worker's paycheck. Now it accounts for 15% and it is expected to continue to rise. This would mean that for every $1,000 of income that an Xer's grandfather earned, he would have been required to pay only $20 into Social Security. For an Xer earning that same amount today he will have to pay over $150.[36] "In 1990, a couple in their twenties with one worker, a baby, and $30,000 in income had to pay five times as much tax to the government ($5,055) as the typical retired couple in their late sixties with the same income from public and private pensions ($1,073)."[37]

All of this seems unfair to the Xer. But then, that doesn't surprise him all that much because most of his life has been unfair. That is why he is typically pessimistic towards the future and feels no obligations towards society or any of its rules or expectations. He has been abandoned to work things out on his own, so that is what he will do, and what works will be his bottom line. He is a pragmatist to the end.

Life Application and Implication For Ministry

1. The members of Generation X like to be involved, but they prefer to serve on an individual and personal level rather than in a group. Look over the opportunities for service that your church and youth program offers. Are you providing sufficient opportunities for individual involvement? What are

some additional opportunities that you could add?

2. Do your children or members of your youth group believe in absolutes or do they believe in situation ethics? Develop and administer your own poll to your youth group and discuss the implications of your findings. For some sample questions see: Josh McDowell's *Right From Wrong* and George Barna's *Baby Busters* and *Generation Next*.

3. Do your teens believe that Jesus is the only way to heaven or do they believe that other religions may be just as valid? Can they defend the Christian claim that Christ is the only way? Discuss the implications of John 14:6 and Acts 4:12.

4. Take a poll. Would your teens identify themselves as "Liberal," "Moderate," or "Conservative?" Which political party do they support? "Republican," "Independent," or "Democrat?" After totaling up their responses, have several different issues to vote on and see if the group votes according to their overall position or if they change their position depending upon the particular issue. Try voting on such issues as: abortion, gay rights, homeless, environment, military budget, education and welfare.

5. Look into sponsoring or attending a "True Love Waits" rally. If you are unable to attend, show the video series. It is excellent.

6. What do you think are the key sources of stress for your teens? Compare your answers to the teens themselves. In what ways is the church able to help them cope? Consider a discussion and application of Matthew 6:25-34.

7. How many of your teens have part-time jobs? How does this affect family schedules? Church and youth group? Discuss implications of financial accountability to God and to those in need. Suggest sponsoring a child through World Vision or some other Christian agency.

Notes

1. Douglas Coupland, *Life After God* (New York: Pocket Books, 1994), 273-274.

2. William Mahedy & Janet Bernardi, *A Generation Alone*, 54.

3. George Barna, *Baby Busters*, 69.

4. Geoffrey T. Holtz, *Welcome to the Jungle*, 71.

5. Neil Howe and Bill Strauss, *13th Gen*, 31.

6. Mahedy & Bernardi, *A Generation Alone*, 131.

7. Barna, *Baby Busters*, 81-82.

8. Kevin Graham Ford, *Jesus For a New Generation*, 53-54.

9. Barna, *Baby Busters*, 69.

10. Rowland Nethaway, "Missing Core Values," Cox News Service appearing in the *Hamilton (OH) Journal-News*, 3 November 1993, quoted in Josh McDowell & Bob Hostetler, *Right From Wrong: What You Need to Know to Help Youth Make Right Choices* (Dallas: Word Publishing, 1994), 5.

11. Ford, *Jesus For a New Generation*, 136.

12. Ibid., 137.

13. George Barna, *Generation Next: What Every Parent and Youthworker Needs to Know About the Attitudes and Beliefs of Today's Youth* (Glendale, CA: Barna Research Group, 1995), 58.

14. Ibid., 78.

15. Ibid., 57.

16. Ford, *Jesus For a New Generation*, 187.

17. Rob Nelson & Jon Cowan, *Revolution X: A Survival Guide For Our Generation* (New York: Penguin Books, 1994), xv.

18. Ibid., xix.

19. Ibid., 20.

20. Barna, *Baby Busters*, 124.

21. Howe & Strauss, *13th Gen*, 161.

22. Ford, *Jesus For a New Generation*, 59.

23. Josh McDowell & Dick Day, *Why Wait?: What You Need to Know About the Teen Sexuality Crisis* (San Bernardino, CA: Here's Life Publishers, 1987), 22-23.

24. Howe & Strauss, *13th Gen*, 148.

25. Barna, *Baby Busters*, 122.

26. Ibid., 124.

27. Mahedy & Bernardi, *A Generation Alone*, 95.

28. Ibid., 97.

29. Barna, *Baby Busters*, 124.

30. Barna, *Generation Next*, 13.

31. Ibid., 24.

32. See Mahedy & Bernardi, *A Generation Alone*, 13-29.

33. "Earnings on the Job." *The Youth Ministry Resource Book* (Loveland, CO: Group Books, 1988), 87.

34. William Dunn, *The Baby Bust: A Generation Comes of Age.* (Ithaca, NY: American Demographics Books, 1993), 122.

35. Nelson & Cowan, *Revolution X*, 109.

36. Ibid., 66-67.

37. U.S. Congress, Ways and Means Committee staff report. Quoted in Howe & Strauss, 96.

Overview and Summary

My generation is an emotional basket case. As a class, our self-esteem is low. The prevalence of body art (tattoos) on both young men and young women suggests a lack of self-respect and self-esteem. To Xers the body is no longer a temple. It is just another bare wall upon which to scrawl our graffiti. — Kevin Graham Ford in *Jesus For A New Generation*[1]

The difference was that dysfunctionality and trauma had never before been the *prevailing* conditions for most American youngsters. What had once been considered unusual or aberrant behavior now seemed to have become the norm. — William Mahedy & Janet Bernardi in *A Generation Alone*[2]

Thirteeners are cursed with the lowest collective self-esteem of any youth generation in living memory. Every new crop of Americans comes of age facing its share of family problems, adolescent agonies, and spoiled dreams. But none other this century has felt anything like the 13ers' collective sense of missionlessness — of feeling worthless, wasted, even despised as a group. Of wondering why they were even born. — Neil Howe & Bill Strauss in *13th Gen: Abort, Retry, Ignore, Fail?*[3]

Adolescence in America has become a deadly minefield, and increasing numbers of young people are not making it through. Some perish along the way — killing themselves, murdering one another or dying in accidents. Others emerge wounded, bearing physical or emotional scars that they will carry for the rest of their lives. — Ronald Kotulak in *Growing Up At Risk: Dangerous Passage*[4]

Generation X has proven to be the most unwanted generation to make its debut in American history. Their parents took birth control pills not to have them. They are the most aborted of all generations. Ten million became the first latchkey kids. One in three was physically or sexually abused. Over half come from divorced families. Many were neglected by parents in pursuit of

95

their careers. Others have had to make difficult adjustments in blended family situations. A large number grew up in single parent homes without the benefit of a father's care or influence.

School House Woes

They were the recipients of a questionable educational philosophy. The lowest SAT and ACT scores in American history compiled by this generation is evidence to that fact. They didn't learn anything in school and it was outright dangerous just to be there. About 450,000 violent crimes take place in U.S. schools each year.[5] While the quality of their educational preparation plummeted, the cost of a college education soared. The average cost of attending a private college in the 1977-1978 school year was just $5,000. In the 1992-1993 academic year that figure had risen to $18,000. Adjusted for inflation, the total cost for attending a private college rose more than 70% for the Xer.[6]

Soaring Crime

Since 1950 juvenile delinquency has increased by 250% in the United States. While 15- to 24-year olds make up about 20% of the population, they account for roughly half of the nation's arrests.[7] Neil Howe and Bill Strauss predict that Xers will be incarcerated and executed at a higher rate than any previous generation in U.S. History. The number of Xers incarcerated has already increased by 33% from the previous generation.[8] The average sentences for young-adult offenders has nearly doubled. Much of Xer crime tends to be more random, senseless and savage than previous generations. The 1989 "wilding" in New York City where a gang of youth brutally beat, knifed, and raped a 28-year-old woman for no other reason than "it was fun" is a frightening example of this.

From 1985 to 1991 the rate of homicide arrests for teenagers and young adults more than doubled. And, surprisingly, the

96

greatest increase in the overall crime rate was seen by teenager girls, with the number arrested for all violent crimes soaring by 62 percent in a decade.[9]

The first Xers, those born in 1961-1964, set the record for sociopathology among American youth. "They set the all-time U.S. youth records for drunk driving, illicit drug consumption, and suicide. They have been among the most violent, criminal, and heavily-incarcerated youth cohorts in U.S. History."[10] One of every four black American males between the ages of 20 and 29 is currently in prison, on probation, or on parole. In Washington, D.C. 42% of all black men ages 18-35 are either in prison, under court supervision, or sought for arrest; 70% are arrested at least once before they reach age 35.[11]

Stress, Suicide and Mental Health

While Xers have a much lower risk of dying from a deadly disease than previous generations, they have a much higher risk of dying from accidents, murder or suicide. Adolescent suicide has tripled in the past thirty years. One teenage suicide tragedy strikes every 90 minutes in the United States.[12] While the suicide rate for the rest of the population remained stable, the rate for ages 15-24 rose by 41% between 1970 and 1978.[13] About 73% of teenagers have thought about committing suicide. Of these, 27% have actually tried.[14]

Inpatient hospitalization for children under 18 has increased from 82,000 in 1980 to more than 112,000 in 1986. Most of that increase was in admissions to private hospitals; roughly 43,000 children were admitted to free-standing private psychiatric hospitals in 1986, compared to only 17,000 in 1980 and 6,452 in 1970.[15] The number of Americans between the ages of 10 and 19 discharged from psychiatric units between 1980 and 1987 increased by 43%, from 126,000 to 180,000, according to the National Center for Health Statistics. This figure is all the more striking because the population of that age group shrank by 11% for that same period. About 12% of children under 18, roughly 8 million kids, need mental health services, according to the National Association of private Psychiatric Hospitals.[16]

- Every 78 seconds, an adolescent in this country attempts suicide. Every 90 minutes, one succeeds.
- Every 20 minutes, an adolescent is killed in an accident. Every 80 minutes, one is murdered.
- Every 31 seconds, an adolescent becomes pregnant.
- Nearly half of all high school seniors have used an illegal drug at least once, and almost 90% have used alcohol — some on a daily basis.
- 3.4 million of the nation's 17 million high school students have mental problems — and most are not receiving any help.
- 20% feel emotionally empty and view life as an endless serious of problems without solutions.
- Every 30 seconds a child's parents are divorced.

Source: *Growing Up At Risk: Dangerous Passage*

Sexual Attitudes and Consequences

There has been a serious paradigm shift in the youth culture with reference to sexual involvement. It used to be that a person who was *not* a virgin was the one who was stigmatized. Now virginity seems to bear the stigma that was once attached to premarital sex. It is not uncommon to hear a teen say, "Yeah, I did it last night just to get it over with, so I could say that I have had sex." Amongst Xers there is subtle social pressure — an unspoken expectation as it were, that everyone will become sexually experienced as soon as possible. If you don't, then there must be something wrong with you. You are the oddball if you haven't had sex.

About the only Xers I know who make any efforts at sexual restraint are members of Christian churches, young adult communities and campus fellowships who not only take Christian moral standards seriously but also sense some kind of intrinsic connection between physical sex and the deep personal and public commitment that mature sexuality entails.[17]

While there may be pockets of teens and young adults who still practice purity and are waiting until marriage for their sexual involvement, the accepted norm among Xers seems to be that if you love someone, if you are involved in a relationship, that relationship will automatically include sexual involvement. If they have been raised to believe that there are no absolutes, what reason would they have for not doing so? It is not like they invented the moral standard into which they were born. They inherited it from their anti-establishment, break all the rules Boomer parents. But they have learned to live by it.

This rejection of moral standards in the sexual arena has not been without cost. Two and a half million adolescents a year contracted some form of STD during the eighties.[18] The Guttmacher Institute estimates that of the 12 million new STD infections that strike Americans each year, 8 million of those infected are under the age of twenty-five.[19] Infection rates for gonorrhea alone, tripled among fifteen- to nineteen-year-olds from 1960 to 1988, and quadrupled for those aged ten to fourteen during the same years.[20] In order to truly appreciate the magnitude of the seriousness of this problem, you must understand how widespread STD's are among Generation X when compared to other age groups. The infection rates for gonorrhea in 1991 for teenage boys was six times as high as it was for adults over age thirty, and for teenage girls the rate was twenty-two times as high according to the Centers for Disease Control.[21] Even though the spread of sexually transmitted diseases is at epidemic proportions among teenagers and young adults, there is no indication that there will be any change in their sexual morals or behavior outside of those who undergo a religious conversion.

Over a million teenage girls become pregnant every year. There are 30,000 of them who are under the age of fifteen who give birth.[22] While there have always been pregnancies to unmarried girls down through the ages, there is a difference with Generation X. For previous generations, they would be "unplanned" or "unwanted" pregnancies. But increasing numbers of today's teenage girls are getting pregnant because they *want* to. When asked why they would want to have a baby out of wedlock, most would reply, "Because I wanted someone to love me."

Teenage Runaways and Throwaways

There are over 125,000 teens who are living on the streets because they have been forced out of their homes.[23] These are not runaways by choice, chasing after the "bright lights" of the city, but these are kids who have been abandoned. They are told to leave home for such offenses as misbehaving, getting pregnant or even something as insignificant as eating too much. These kids are "throwaways," pushed out by their parents. According to a 1989 House committee study, if you add together the number the youths who have been placed in foster homes, detention centers and mental health facilities with the number of throwaways, they would total nearly 500,000.[24] Many of these number do not show up on the runaway statistics because they are not reported as missing because no one back home is looking for them. Their parents want them gone and they want them to stay gone.

Because of their lack of marketable skills, most runaways end up involved in prostitution because they have no other way to make money. It is a harsh life. Daily they have to face the threat of STD's, dying of AIDS, or getting physically abused by their pimp or john. Not all survive. In the eighties, an estimated 5,000 kids a year were buried in unmarked graves, unidentified and unmourned.[25]

Trauma and Survivor's Guilt

Overall, Xers seem to be more traumatized by life than any other generation. Yes, there have always been young people who have been raised in hostile environments who have had to deal with poverty, chemically addicted parents, abusive parents or absent parents. There have always been a certain amount of young people who have had to struggle with some serious problems growing up. But the difference between then and now is that dysfunctionality and trauma seem to be the prevailing conditions for today's youth. What was once considered unusual or aberrant behavior has now become the norm.

Even if you have a young person who was raised in a loving, supportive environment by an intact family, that person goes to school and most of his or her friends come from dysfunctional families. A good deal of their interaction together centers around their friends' personal and family problems. The Xer ends up with a sort of warped view of life because he sees it through the prism of his peers' struggles.

I was sharing some of these insights and information about Generation X at a seminar I was leading at the National Youth Leaders Convention in Joplin, MO held on the campus of Ozark Christian College by Christ In Youth. I was making the point about how traumatized Generation X was and how it affected even those who were raised in healthy families. One young college student who identified herself as an Xer, gave me some additional insight. Her parents divorced when she was two and she was raised by her grandparents. They were very loving and supportive people and she grew up in a positive home environment. But when she went to school and listened to her friends share about all of the problems they were experiencing in their own homes, she felt guilty. She felt guilty because her home situation was warm and loving and her friend's homes were fraught with problems. In order to fit in, she even went out of her way to look for something wrong or start a fight with her grandmother just so she could go to school and be able to complain about life and her family like everyone else.

She was experiencing a form of "survivor's guilt." Survivor's guilt is common in those who survive different catastrophes such as natural disasters like floods, tornadoes, earthquakes and hurricanes. It is also found among the survivors of plane crashes and other accidents. The person who lives feels guilty about his survival when so many around him died or were seriously injured. He does not feel worthy of his fortune, especially if he was close friends or a relative of some of the other victims. The result is an overall depression and sense of guilt over being the one who survived. This is the reason for some of the despair and hopelessness found among Generation X, even if they were not personally abused or traumatized in any way. It is guilt by association.

Hostility

There is a tremendous amount of pent-up rage and hostility with Generation X. They are angry and bitter about how they have been treated and let down by those whom they have trusted the most. As my good friend and colleague Mark Moore told me, "I was shafted by the three p's — parents, preachers and politicians." You must understand, his parents divorced when he was just entering his teens. His preacher had an affair and devastated the church, and Richard Nixon had resigned from the White House in shame. All of the key authority figures in his life let him down.

His response was a typical Xer response. He became fiercely independent and trusted no one but himself. He became a survivor. Only by the grace of Jesus has he been able to overcome the bitterness and learn to open up and trust again. He is now married and has a wonderful relationship with his wife and children. He is also an excellent teacher, one who cares very deeply for his students. He is involved in their lives and shares deeply from his own. He stands as a testimony to the fact that those who have been deeply wounded can be whole once again. Mark is one of the fortunate ones. His faith saw him through. Most are not that lucky.

Xers are also angry about their bleak economic future. There are fewer jobs that pay well. Most that do pay well require a college education and the costs of a four year degree have soared in the past twenty years. Even if they do get a degree, there is no guarantee that they will be fortunate enough to secure one of the better paying positions.

I was asked to do a seminar on Generation X at the 1995

North American Christian Convention in Indianapolis, IN. As I was leaving the motel and pulling onto the main street that led to the convention center I was passed by an old, brown, rusted out Toyota Celica. Driving it was a young teenager, dressed in the familiar uniform and hat of a major fast-food restaurant chain. On the rear of his car was a bumper sticker which said it all, "Die Yuppie Scum!"

Darkness On The Horizon

Because of all of the problems that have surrounded their lives, most Xers do not feel very optimistic about the future. They share a dark cynicism and hopelessness about life. A 1993 Gallup poll found that one in three members of Generation X believe he or she would be shot to death before reaching old age.[26] For the Xer, life is a ride on the Titanic. Since it is fated to sink and there is nothing you can do about it, then the best that you can do is to go first class.

This hopelessness is one of the reasons why so many of them ignore the warnings about the dangers of drug abuse or promiscuous sex. From their standpoint, it's all just a matter of time anyway. So they live "on the edge" hoping to get the most out of life before their time is up. An incredible illustration of this is seen in the responses of one hundred young track-and-field athletes to a question posed to them by Dr. Gabe Mirkin. He asked them, "If I could give you a drug that would make you an Olympic champion, but would kill you a year later, would you take it?" To his disbelief, more than half of the athletes answered "yes."[27] You see, for Generation X, there is no assurance of tomorrow. All they have is "now" and they will do whatever it takes to make the present the best that it can be. It is all they have got.

Are There Any Exceptions?

I would be remiss if I did not point out that there are pockets of hope to be found within Generation X. Abilene Christian University researchers Dr. David Lewis and Dr. Carley Dodd studied a nationwide survey of the beliefs and attitudes of over 1,000 senior high and middle school teenagers in the churches of Christ. What they found was that many of their respondents held great hope for the future and felt good about themselves, but did not believe that their fellow Xers were as optimistic. They found:

- ✠ 75% of senior high students view their generation as depressed while only 22% report experiencing depression themselves.
- ✠ 72% of high schoolers say Generation Xers are addicted to media while only 24% claim to be addicted themselves.
- ✠ 83% of high schoolers said they feel safe inside their families, but predicted only 25% of Generation Xers would feel secure in theirs.[28]

As with the case of my good friend Mark mentioned earlier, a personal faith in God and involvement in a church has made a difference in the life of an Xer. The optimism of those surveyed by Lewis and Dodd came from their commitment to Christ. But even though they had hope, they recognized that most of their friends would not feel as optimistic about their own personal lives or the future.

In the January 1995 issue of *Reader's Digest*, there appeared an exclusive article entitled "Exposing the Myth of the Generation Gap."[29] In this article they revealed the results of a poll taken from a scientific sampling of 1053 Americans comparing the fundamental beliefs and values of four generations. To their surprise, what they found was most Americans, regardless of their age, still share some common ideals and beliefs about life.

Comparing the Beliefs of Four Generations				
	Depression Era (63+)	Silents (49-62)	Boomers (31-48)	Xers (18-30)
Hard work is the key to getting ahead.	78%	66%	75%	74%
Unlimited opportunity is more important than ensuring greater equality of income.	69%	78%	74%	72%
Big government poses the greatest threat to the nation's future.	63%	66%	70%	70%
They are generally satisfied in their personal lives.	83%	85%	87%	81%
Volunteerism: Have done volunteer work to help others.	45%	54%	59%	50%
Faith: Have always believed in God.	92%	88%	87%	87%
Source: *Reader's Digest*				

What does this mean? Does it invalidate all of the other information? I would have to say that it does not invalidate the other information, but does serve to give us hope. Even in the midst of the darkest of times, there are always rays of hope. Bright spots. For the most part this information does not really contradict anything that has been written about the personal experiences of Generation X. Rather it affirms most of what has already been said. Hard work and opportunity would fit right in to their pragmatic worldview. If it works, if it is practical, if it gives them a sense of autonomy as opposed to depending upon the system or others, Xers are going to be in favor of it. They are already upset at big government because of the huge national debt that they have inherited from the preceding generations. As was stated in an earlier chapter, Xers are very much service oriented — they just do it differently than previous generations. Xers prefer to serve individually and quietly rather than in groups with a media parade documenting their every move. While Xers did indicate that a high percent believe in God, I would have to ask, "Which God?" Certainly it is not the Judeo-Christian God of their grandparents. A typical Xer is just as likely to call some nebulous, Star Wars-like force his god. Xers *are* very spiritual. It is just that their spirituality is more of the do-it-yourself kind. They borrow a little bit here and a little

105

bit there and put it all together to construct their own religious experience and their own view of God. When comparing the beliefs between the generations, one must first make sure that the words mean the same thing to the people involved.

In conclusion, I would like to say that in spite of all the problems and the darkness surrounding Generation X, I have great hopes for this generation. They have the potential to be the X of the equation, the unknown quantity which provides the solution to many of the problems facing our nation and culture today. As a member of the Boomer generation, I believe that we owe them an apology for the way we put our jobs and careers before them. We need to apologize for having opened the floodgates to the problems stemming from promiscuous sex, illegal drug use, and the breakdown of all morals. We have polluted the environment and created a huge debt which we expect them to pay.

Rather than casting aspersions at them and labeling them "a generation of slackers," we should seek to understand them and help them find their place in the world. After all, we helped to create them. They are the product of their times as was the generation before them and the generation before them. In order to better understand how the phenomenon of Generation X came about, we must look at the historical and philosophical developments of the years preceding them. Many of the foundational events and key issues which helped to create the world of Generation X are the direct result of a cultural paradigm shift. Western Christian civilization has moved away from a modern worldview to a post-modern one. It is the post-modern culture which has given birth to Generation X. In the next section we will examine the history of Generation X and seek to better understand the forces and philosophies which contributed to their birth.

DIFFERENCES BETWEEN BOOMERS AND GENERATION X		
	Boomer	**Generation X**
Sexual Disease	Herpes	AIDS
TV Evangelist	Billy Graham	Jimmy Swaggart
Movie Villain	Norman Bates	Freddy Krueger
Gang Movie	*West Side Story*	*Colors*
Youth Culture Movie	*The Graduate*	*The Breakfast Club*
Popular Street Drug	Pot	Crack
Dance Craze	The Twist	Slam Dancing
Music Innovation	Rock-N-Roll	Rap
NASA Memory	Apollo 11 Moon Landing	Space Shuttle Challenger Explosion
Political Memory	Cuban Missile Crisis	Resignation of Richard Nixon
Video Game	Pong	Mortal Kombat
Rock Group	The Beatles	Nirvana
What Do You Want To Be When You Grow Up?	Fireman, Policemen, Nurse	Alive
Musical Instrument	Transistor Radio	Portable CD Player
Political Cause	Civil Rights	Gay Rights
Late Night TV	Johnny Carson	David Letterman
Political Loyalties	Left vs Right	Post Partisan
Information Source	Newspaper	Internet
Philosophical Base	Ideological	Pragmatic
Female Musician	Joan Baez	Madonna
War	Cold War	Regional Wars
National Threat	Nuclear Threat	Terrorist Threats
Nurture	Mother's Care	Day Care
Father	"Father Knows Best"	Absent Father
Food	TV Dinners	Low-fat Fast Food
Television	Network TV	Cable TV
Music Medium	45's & American Bandstand	CD's and MTV & VH1

Life Application and Implication For Ministry

1. Is home schooling the answer to the educational problems facing the nation? What about those who are not able to home school? What advantages are there in sending a child to a private Christian school? Are there any disadvantages? What can parents and concerned community members do

to improve the quality of public education? Perhaps your church or youth group could set up a tutoring service after school as an outreach ministry to the community. The tutoring ministry could be combined with a small snack, some games and a Bible devotion besides the help with individual studies and homework assignments.

2. Take a poll of the teenagers in your church, youth group or Sunday School. Determine how many struggle with an inordinate amount of stress in their lives. Hold a seminar on "Cognitive Restructuring" to help them learn some constructive ways of coping with stress. I would highly recommend the excellent book on cognitive restructuring by Chris Thurman entitled: *The Lies We Believe.*

3. What is being done in your community to help with the problem of teenage runaways or throwaways? Is there a runaway hotline number that they could call if they were in trouble? Are the students and sponsors aware of it? Have a student do a presentation on the history and ministry of Covenant House. Perhaps your youth group or Sunday School could pledge to support Covenant House with a monthly offering.

Notes

1. Kevin Graham Ford, *Jesus For A New Generation*, 25.

2. William Mahedy & Janet Bernardi, *A Generation Alone*, 22.

3. Neil Howe & Bill Strauss, *13th Gen*, 85.

4. Ronald Kotulak, "Growing Up At Risk: Dangerous Passage," *Chicago Tribune*, 7 December 1986, Sec 6 p.1.

5. Mark Mayfield, "Assaults Top the List of Classroom Chaos," *USA Today*, 8 December, 1986, p. 10A.

6. Geoffrey T. Holtz, *Welcome to the Jungle*, 122-123.

7. Eugene C. Roehlkepartain, *The Youth Ministry Resource Book*, 169.

8. William Strauss & Neil Howe, *Generations*, 326.

9. Holtz, *Welcome to the Jungle*, 96.

10. Howe & Strauss, *13th Gen*, 88.

11. The Washington Post, quoted in Howe & Strauss.

12. Jerry Johnston, *Why Suicide?* (New York: Oliver Nelson, 1987), 34.

13. Finley H. Sizemore, *Suicide: The Signs and Solutions* (Wheaton, IL: Victor Books, 1988), 9.

14. Teenage Magazine survey, reported in "Teenagers Think About Suicide," *Group*, September 1987, 21.

15. Nina Darnton, "Committed Youth," *Newsweek*, 31 July 1989, 66-72.

16. The Wall Street Journal.

17. Mahedy & Bernardi, *A Generation Alone*, 101.

18. Warren E. Leary, "Gloomy Report on the Health of Teenagers," *New York Times*, 9 June 1990, 24.

19. Felicity Barringer, "Report Finds 1 in 5 Infected by Viruses Spread Sexually," *New York Times*, 1 April 1993, p. A1.

20. Daniel Goleman, "Teen-Agers Called Shrewd Judges of Risk," *New York Times*, 1 March 1993, p. B5.

21. "Health Report," *Time*, 30 August 1993, 16.

22. Claudia Wallis, "Children Having Children," *Time*, 9 December 1985, 78-90.

23. Martin Forst and Martha-Elin Blomquist. *Missing Children: Rhetoric and Reality*, 42, cited in Holtz, *Welcome to the Jungle*, 93.

24. Rich Spencer, "'Discarded' Child Population Put at Nearly 500,000," *Washington Post* 12 December 1989, A1.

25. "Throwaway Kids." *Newsweek*, 25 April 1988, 65.

26. Cited in "Harper's Index," *Harper's Magazine*, February 1994, 13.

27. Bob Goldman, *Death In The Locker Room* (South Bend, IN: Icarus, 1984), 32.

28. Malissa Endsley, "Understanding Generation X," *ACU Today*, Spring 1995, 12.

29. Everett C. Ladd, "Exposing the Myth of the Generation Gap," *Reader's Digest*, January 1995, 49-54.

SECTION 2

Understanding the History of Generation X

Worldview

All ages, the modern era included, are shaped by great ideas. Political and economic systems, religious beliefs, philosophies, cultural assumptions and knowledge of the natural world are always interrelated, and within a culture they coalesce to form some sort of cohesive world view. — William Mahedy & Janet Bernardi in *A Generation Alone*[1]

A profound shift in thinking has taken place in the space of a generation. Generation X is the first to see the world through post-modern eyes. Very few of those who were born prior to Generation X understand how radically the thought patterns of Xers differ from their own ways of thinking. The ground has shifted under the feet of the Baby Boomers, and they don't even know it. My generation doesn't just look and dress and act differently from previous generations. My generation truly thinks differently, perceives differently, believes differently and processes truth differently from any previous generation. — Kevin Graham Ford in *Jesus For a New Generation*[2]

A new day has dawned. A new generation has come of age. The new generation is post-Christian, post-Enlightenment, and postmodern. The church is faced with a new challenge. The previous generation of church leaders responded to the rationalistic, atheistic challenge of the claim that there is no God. But for postmoderns the question is not "Is there a God?" but "Which God?" — David S. Dockery in *The Challenge of Postmodernism*[3]

One cannot explore or try to understand the phenomenon of Generation X without understanding the basic tenets and influence of postmodern philosophy. Postmodernism has affected the arts, values, morals, communication, music and thought processes of Generation X. Xers are the first generation to bring postmodern assumptions to all aspects of life. This change represents a complete paradigm shift in the way that they perceive reality and have come to understand truth. Some see this shift as being as radical as the previous shift from theism to rationalism. But before looking at the specifics of postmodernism, it is best to look at the ideas and historical events which led up to the development of postmodern thought.

Postmodernism is a worldview. What is a worldview? James W. Sire writes:

> A worldview is a set of presuppositions (or assumptions) which we hold (consciously or subconsciously) about the basic makeup of our world.
>
> . . . A worldview is composed of a number of basic presuppositions, more or less self-consistent, generally unquestioned by each person, rarely, if even, mentioned by his friends, and only brought to mind when challenged by a foreigner from another ideological universe.[4]

A worldview gives one answers to the basic questions about life, existence and meaning. It would answer questions about what is "prime reality" or that which is really real. It would provide answers to epistemological questions, i.e., how does one discover or know truth? How does one know *at all*, and how does one *know* that he knows?

A worldview answers all of the most pertinent questions concerning man's existence: 1) Who is man? 2) Where did he come from? 3) Where is he going? 4) How should he conduct himself in day to day matters and in relationship with others? How does one seek answers to basic morality issues? 5) What is the meaning of human history? Does it have a purpose or is it meaningless?

A worldview is concerned with the nature and makeup of reality. Is it made up only of primary bits of matter, or is there an unseen, non-material substance that is just as much a part of reality, though unobserved, such as a spirit or soul?

Spiritual questions would be a part of one's worldview. Is there really a God? If there is, how would you learn about him or know him? What is his character? Is he involved in the affairs of men? If so, in what way?

The Theistic Worldview

For seventeen centuries the common worldview of Western man was that of theism. Theism is the worldview which declares that the prime reality of the universe is the Judeo-Christian God as revealed in the Bible. This God is Triune (three in one) and he has revealed himself to man, both through creation (Rom 1:19-20; Ps 19:1-2) and through revelation (John 1:1-3, 14; Heb 1:1-2). Thus, God has revealed himself to man both through general or natural revelation and special revelation.

The Judeo-Christian God is a personal God. He is a being with personality and cannot be reduced down to some impersonal "force" as seen in *Star Wars*. He is much more than energy. He is the only self-existent being (Exod 3:14).

God is also transcendent and immanent. To be transcendent means that God is beyond the limits of ordinary experience. He is beyond the limits of all possible experience and knowledge; he is above the seen and material universe. But this does not mean that God is absent from his creation or uninvolved in the affairs of man. God is immanent in his creation, that is, "he is here, everywhere, in a sense completely in line with his transcendence."[5] God is present everywhere in the universe, and yet he stands apart from it in the essential nature of his being. God is a Spirit and it is the presence and power of his Spirit that sustains the universe (Col 1:16-17).

God is omniscient and sovereign. He is all powerful and all-knowing. He is the ultimate source of all knowledge and all intelligence. As the sovereign Lord of the universe nothing is beyond God's ultimate control, authority and desire. In fact, Psalm 139:13-16 expresses the fact that God knows every individual even before they are born. He knows everyone of their deeds even before any one of them has taken place.

God is also infinitely just, holy and good. All of his actions are totally righteous. There is no shadow of turning or hint of evil in his character. All of his interactions with mankind are fair and just. Everything that God does within creation is for the ultimate good of mankind.

God is the creator of the universe and all that is found within it, both living beings and inanimate objects. He created it all *ex nihilo* (out of nothing) for his glory. It speaks of his power and wonder (Ps 19:1). Because God is a purposeful God, the universe that he created runs according to purpose. It has meaning.

> The universe was a creation of meaning. Meaning is intrinsic to reality. It is not something a man makes up when he does his scientific study. It is something he discovers or something that is revealed to him; it is something that is there whether or not man is there or whether or not man recognizes it.[6]

The universe is also orderly. God is an orderly being and it is only fitting that his creation reflect his nature and not chaos and confusion. The universe is the way it is, at least in part, because of who God is. It reflects his nature.

Genesis tell us that God created man and woman in "his own image" and "after his likeness."[7] According to the Western religious view man is to be understood primarily from the standpoint of his divine origin.

> His uniqueness is not chiefly in his reason or in his relation to nature. Man is a being created by God and made in God's image. Man stands at the point where nature and spirit meet. The fact that man is a finite creature, bound to the earth, explains his weakness and his sinfulness. The fact that man is in part a spiritual being who transcends nature explains his uniqueness, worth, and almost unlimited possibilities.[8]

The two main texts supporting the western religious view of man are Genesis 1:26-27 and 2:7. In 2:7 the Bible says, "The Lord God formed the man from the dust of the ground and breathed into his nostrils the breath of life, and the man became a living being." Some translations say ". . . living soul." When translated in this way, it does not mean soul in the usual sense, but an animated being and is a description of man as a whole. "The very same Hebrew term, *nephesh chayyah* (living soul or being) is also applied to the animals in Genesis 1:21, 24, 30."[9]

Genesis 1:26-27 says:

> Then God said, "Let us make man in our image in our likeness, and let them rule over the fish of the sea and the birds of the air, over the livestock, over all the earth, and over all the creatures that move along the ground." So God created man in his own image, in the image of God he created him; male and female he created them.

Man's uniqueness from all other creation is that he alone is created "in the image of God," the *imago dei*. This uniqueness is stamped upon both the male and the female. While the Bible is clear that mankind has the divine stamp of the *imago dei*, it does not elaborate or define further exactly what this term means. Much speculation has been given down through the centuries.

Some have interpreted the *imago dei* as referring to man's "original righteousness," his having possession of true knowledge, righteousness and holiness before the fall and the corrupting influence of sin. In this sense one would say the *imago dei* was the equivalent of the "moral image of God."

Not wanting to limit the *imago dei* to just the original knowledge, righteousness and holiness which was lost by sin, others have interpreted it as describing the elements which belong to the natural constitution of man.

> They are elements which belong to man as man, such as intellectual power, natural affections, and moral freedom. As created in the image of God man has a rational and moral nature, which he did not lose by sin and which he could not lose without ceasing to be man. This part of the image of God has indeed been vitiated by sin, but still remains in man even after his fall in sin. Notice that man even after the fall, irrespective of his spiritual condition, is still represented as the image of God, Gen 9:6; I Cor 11:7; Jas 3:9.[10]

God is Spirit so it is also assumed that there must be a spiritual dimension in man as the image of God. Indeed, the New

117

Testament acknowledges the spiritual aspect of man. It is often represented as being in opposition to the flesh (Matt 26:41; Rom 7:14-25; 8:1-14). While man must struggle with the flesh, it is a great mistake to fall into the Greek error of seeing the flesh as totally bad and only the spiritual as good. The Biblical view of man is always a wholistic one.

Still another aspect of the *imago dei* is the immortality of man. Man is not immortal like God in the sense of possessing immortality as an essential quality, never having a beginning and having no end. But God endowed man with immortality (Rom 2:7; I Cor 15:53-55).

One of the most accepted interpretations of the image of God has been that it resides in man's capacity to reason. Human rationality is a participation in and reflection of the divine logos or reason by which the world was created.

A related but different interpretation of the *imago dei* has to do with man's authority and dominion over the earth. Humanity resembles God in that it exercises power and dominion over the other creatures.

Another view is that the image of God has to do with human freedom. Man is a free, self-determining, and self-transcending creature. He has the capacity to create. Man can create works of art with his hands, poetry with the pen and culture with his laws and organization.

One last idea is that the image of God describes human life in relationship with God and other creatures. Since God desires and seeks to be in relationship to man and created both male and female it would seem that one of the essential aspects of being created in the image of God is to be in relationship.

However one interprets the *imago dei* in the original man, there must be some kind of altering of that original perception because of original sin. In that original act of disobedience, something profound and disastrous happened to the human race (Rom 5:12-21). Just exactly what happened and the extent of it has been the center of religious controversy for centuries.

The realistic view interprets the fall as having the whole

human race potentially and numerically present in the loins of Adam. Just as Aaron paid tithes to Melchizedek by being in the loins of Abraham according to Hebrews 7:9-10, so all mankind participated in the original sin.

The representative view sees Adam as the federal head of the human race. He was man's representative. When Adam sinned, he sinned not just for himself, but as the representative for all mankind.

Augustine and Calvin emphasized the corruption of the *imago dei.* They saw man as becoming totally depraved because of original sin. This depravity wiped out the stamp of the image of God. As a result, man passes on a totally corrupt nature to his offspring. Not only does all mankind suffer the effects or consequences of Adam's sin, a corrupt nature, but also the guilt of Adam's sin.

The view of Pelagius is that every man born into the world has the same nature as did Adam in the garden. He has freedom of choice and can choose to do the good. The only effect Adam has on the human race is that of a bad example. While Calvin's view seems too harsh, the Pelagian view is too optimistic. It does not do justice to many of the Romans texts, and seems to ignore the universal experience of the sinfulness of man.

The Arminian view teaches that all mankind receive a corrupted nature both physically and intellectually from Adam, but that God at birth gives the Holy Spirit to counteract this corruption. But, even with the aid of the Spirit, each person chooses to do evil and therefore ratifies Adam's sin in their own life.

The New School theory teaches that man is born with a corrupt nature, but that this nature is not totally corrupt. The inherent tendency to sin is there, but this tendency is not the equivalent of being accountable for the guilt of Adam's original sin. Man still retains his freedom of choice, but inevitably chooses to sin.

Whatever view one chooses, there is no denying that Adam's original transgression adversely affected the nature of man. It is my opinion that the fall did not totally wipe out the *imago dei*, that there is still the divine image stamped upon the essential makeup of every man and woman. However, the fall did so corrupt the nature of man so as to pass on to each and every person an inherent tendency toward sin. This tendency is so strong that everyone will choose to sin (Rom 3:10-18, 23), and only in being made new by the transforming power of Christ can man ever hope to overcome and be victorious in this struggle.

While it is true that man has a fallen nature, that he is not all that he once was in his original state in the Garden of Eden, the Judeo-Christian view of man still is one of dignity. The Psalmist speaks of the valued place that man has in creation. Keep in mind that this was written about man even after the fall.

> When I consider your heavens, the work of your fingers, the moon and the stars, which you have set in place, what is man that you are mindful of him, the son of man that you care for him? You made him a little lower than the heavenly beings and crowned him with glory and honor. You made him ruler over the works of your hands; you put everything under his feet: all flocks and herds, and the beasts of the field, the birds of the air, and the fish of the sea, all that swim the paths of the seas.[11]

Theism teaches that man has an ultimate destiny — it is either heaven or hell. Physical death does not bring about the annihilation of man. His spirit and soul continue to exist even after the physical body has ceased to function or even to exist. The sovereign God has set aside a day in which he will call up from the graves all who have ever lived, both the righteous and the unrighteous. Everyone will be judged according to what he has done (John 5:28-29).

Because of this, all history is viewed as linear — it has purpose and direction. It is a meaningful sequence of events which are leading up to God's ultimate destiny for mankind — the judgment, heaven or hell. Historical events are not just random, meaningless, unconnected acts, but a part of the continuing drama that God is directing in his creation. History has meaning because the God of the universe is behind all events working them out for his good pleasure and will.

> History is not reversible, not repeatable, not cyclic; history is not meaningless. Rather, history is teleological, going somewhere, directed toward a known end. The God who knows the end from the beginning is aware of and sovereign over the actions of mankind.[12]

Theism teaches that there is an absolute moral standard by which all people are to live. This standard is revealed to man in the Bible. It is the expression of God's holy and just character. It is seen in the Ten Commandments, the Beatitudes, and the ethical instructions found in Paul's letters. It permeates the historical account of God's dealings with his people. The ultimate revelation of God's standard, however, is found in the life of his one and only son, Jesus Christ, who lived, died and rose again to redeem mankind (Heb 1:1-3).

The Modern Worldview

The theistic worldview was the predominant philosophical influence for seventeen centuries. One might wonder what happened to cause it to lose favor or influence if it satisfactorily answered all of man's basic questions? Why did another worldview even develop? What caused people to abandon theism?

In answer to the previous questions, I would have to say that it wasn't just one event or change, but the combination of a number of shifts in thinking which facilitated the move. The first shift was a change from the theistic view to a deistic view of the universe. This first shift had to do with the location of authority for discovering knowledge about God. Under theism the authority for discovering and learning about God was the Bible, special divine revelation. In the deistic worldview, the mind or reason became the center of authority for discovering truth.

During the first seventeen centuries study focused upon God as revealed in the Scriptures. God was considered the source of all knowledge and wisdom, and the person seeking to be wise would seek out God and his wisdom. Gradually, during the beginning years of the "enlightenment" and the dawn of the modern age, man began to study creation. It was reasoned that since God created the universe, and since God is a rational and orderly God, then it seemed logical that his orderliness and character would be reflected in his creation. Creation would bear the stamp of the divine, and by studying "nature" or creation, man would learn about God.

While it is true that God is revealed in nature, modern man made the mistake of denying the importance and place of revelation in learning about God and man. He cast out Scripture as the authority and substituted the methodology of science and the application of human reason and logic as his authority on matters of truth. As Peter Medawar has said, "The 17th-century doctrine of the *necessity* of reason was slowly giving way to a belief in the *sufficiency* of reason."[13] Modern man would soon come to acknowledge God only as he could be seen and found in nature through the scientific method.

In rejecting Scripture as the source for authority and relying only upon reason and observation for the means of discovering truth, several major changes came about in modern man's worldview. The first change was in his view of God and his relationship to the creation. Modern man developed a "clockwork" view of God and the universe. This view taught that God was a transcendent God, and that he created the universe but then he left it to run on its own. In other words, God was transcendent in that he had the power and greatness to bring about the creation, but that he was not immanent, not personally involved in the daily affairs of men and his creation. He created the universe much like winding up a clock, and then left it to run on its own according to the rules and laws that he mandated should govern it.

In this view man's concept of God is changed to that of a transcendent force or energy, a Prime Mover or First Cause but not a personal being. God is not involved in his creation, he does not care for it, nor does he love it. He has no personal relationship to it at all. He is distant, removed, foreign and alien.

This belief also affected how man viewed day to day life. If God created the world and then left it to run on its own, if he is not immanent in the world, then there is no possibility for God to enter in to the daily affairs of man and change or alter what is. In other words, miracles would not be possible. A miracle means that God has to enter into the events of man and history and supersede or temporarily suspend some natural law that he has set down for the universe to follow, i.e. parting of the Red Sea, walking on water, raising the dead, or providing manna to eat.

Another way the deistic worldview affected thinking was in man's view of himself. In this view, man is just a part of the clockwork. True, man is personal, he is different from the other elements of the created world, he is not a rock or a tree, but he is still locked into a closed system. He has no way to develop a personal relationship with God and know about the uniqueness of his creation. Without a personal relationship to God, man has no way to transcend this world order. He is just another cog in the machine. He has no hope, no way of ever becoming anything different or more than what he is.

Deism very easily evolved into naturalism. In theism, God is the creator and sustainer of the universe. He is at once both transcendent and immanent in creation. He is a personal God who is very much concerned and involved in the everyday affairs of people. In deism, God is one step removed. He is still transcendent in that he is greater than the creation. He caused it to come into being, but then he removed himself from it. He is no longer immanent, actively involved in the day to day events of history. One could say that God loses his personality in deism. He no longer has a personal relationship with mankind, but is distant and removed. In naturalism, God is further removed — right out the door! God loses his very existence.

In naturalism, matter is what is eternal, not God. Since in the deistic worldview God was not needed for the everyday func-

123

tions of life, but only to give life a start, it was reasoned that God was not needed even for that. Let matter be considered eternal and time and chance the forces which combine together to create life. With this presupposition about life, then man is also further reduced. He is no longer personal or unique, but just matter like all of the other things in the universe.

> The point is that man is simply a part of the cosmos. In the cosmos there is one substance — matter. Man is that and only that. The laws applying to matter apply to him. He does not transcend the universe in any way.[14]

The ultimate implication of this belief is that death is the end of man. He has no soul, no spirit that will go on living eternally, but all that he once was ceases to be. Death is the extinction of personality and individuality. As the *Humanist Manifesto II* states, "As far as we know the total personality is a function of the biological organism transacting in a social and cultural context. There is no credible evidence that life survives the death of the body."[15]

History is seen as a linear stream of events determined by cause and effect, but having no ultimate purpose. Since it has no inherent goal, history is what men make it to be. Human events only have meaning if man ascribes meaning to them. There is no ultimate goal, no destiny awaiting man, only death. Man came from matter and returns to matter.

But this awareness is too painful for man; he wants to survive somehow. He does not want to have extinction be his ultimate end. Ernest Becker has written a book entitled, *The Denial of Death*, which represents a paradigm shift in the psychoanalytic world.[16] It challenges Freud's view that sex and aggression are the ultimate driving forces in man. Becker postulates that the denial of death is the driving force. Since every person is aware that death is the ultimate enemy, all people try to cheat death — to overcome it in some way. He believes that is the reason why people have children, write poetry, compose music, and build architectural wonders — so that they will in some way continue to live through their creations even after their bodies have long since ceased to function.

I think this points out one of the major failings of the naturalistic worldview. It does not account for man's longing and desire to be more than just evolved matter. The Bible says that God has set eternity in the hearts of men.[17] Man wants *more* than just this world. He longs for eternal life.

With the naturalistic worldview ethics are derived from human experience, they are autonomous and situational. They are constructed out of human need and interest. There are no set rules which apply to everyone in every situation, there is no absolute truth because there is no absolute being and no absolute purpose or destiny for life. Therefore, every individual is left to determine his values for himself. These are determined by need and the situation in which he finds himself. They may change from situation to situation, depending upon his need.

The naturalist has no other place to go for finding a base for his ethics and morals because he has done away with God and the unseen world. The world is simply the result of random, purposeless combinations of atoms and matter. There is no meaning or direction behind it. It simply exists. This does not provide man with a sense of oughtness. It only is. Ethics are concerned with what ought to be, not just what is. Where can man go to find a basis for his morals?

> Naturalism places man in an ethically relative box. For man to know what values within that box are true values, he needs a measure imposed on it from outside the box; he needs a moral plumbline by which he can evaluate the conflicting moral values he observes in himself and others. But there is nothing outside the box; there is no moral plumbline, no ultimate, non-changing standard of value. Ergo: ethical nihilism.[18]

Nihilism is the dark, hopeless end of natural philosophy. If matter is all that there is, and if there is no ultimate purpose or meaning in the universe, then man has no basis for significance. Existential despair is the result.

125

In order to deal with his despair man creates meaning. He does it by a new definition of reality. Reality consists of two forms, objective and subjective. Objective reality is made up of all of the solid matter in the universe. Subjective reality is the world of the mind, consciousness and awareness. In the objective world, man is nothing more than material substance, no different from the rest of the universe. But in the subjective world of the mind, man can know and be known by other people. It is in relationship that meaning is created. In effect, truth goes from that which is objective and outside of man, to that which is subjective and inside of him. Truth is not so much what a man *knows* or *reasons* as much as it is what he *feels*. Subjective experience becomes the standard for measuring all of life.

Summary

In theism, truth is centered in God. All of reality is explained in relationship to the creator God. He brought forth all of creation — sun, moon, stars, planets and even life itself, and created man in his own image and likeness as the highlight of his creation. Not only did he create man, but he created him for fellowship. God was transcendent, in that he was greater than the created world, but he was also immanent, meaning that he was personally involved in the day to day affairs of man and his world. Truth and ethics were centered in God. God revealed to man what was truth and what was right and wrong behavior through his prophets and through the written word. Man was given freedom and choice so that the worship and devotion that he would return to the creator would be genuine and heartfelt. God did not create man as a robot, but gave him the freedom of personal choice. God has an ultimate destiny for mankind — heaven or hell. Every event in history, every leader and every nation plays a part in the drama that God has designed for this world and all the people in it.

During the early years of the enlightenment, the deistic worldview developed. In this view the focus shifted from revealed truth about God to discovered truth found in the study and observation of creation. Revelation was set aside in preference of reason. Man believed that he could learn about God from the study of God's creation since the creation was a reflection of God. "The goal of the human intellectual quest became that of unlocking the secrets of the universe, in order to master nature for human benefit and create a better world."[19] In his quest for truth, modern man assumed that knowledge was certain, objective, and good, and that such knowledge was obtainable by reason and observation. He placed an unchallenged faith in man's rational capabilities. Man was able to discover truth because he was able to stand apart from being a conditioned participant and was able to view the world as an unconditioned observer.

Not only did modern man believe that knowledge was certain and objective, but he believed that it was inherently good. The assumption of the inherent goodness of knowledge also meant that modern man's outlook was optimistic at first. It was believed that progress was inevitable because with man's knowledge gained through scientific discovery he could educate others and through shared knowledge eventually come to the place where he would free himself from his vulnerability to nature and solve all social ills.

The end result of this was a removal of God from the affairs of man and an elevation of man to the center of reality. Truth became what man could reason or discover. Reality was reduced to the material world. Creation was viewed as a huge clock which God wound up and then left to run on its own according to the laws and rules that he mandated should govern the universe. God was viewed only as the First Cause, but not personally involved in his creation.

Very soon God was removed completely from the picture. Instead of God being the First Cause, the Prime Mover of everything, matter was considered to be eternal and the source of all life. Everything in the universe came about as the result of chance, random processes through millions of years of evolution. Everything in life was simply a combination of the essential ingredients of matter, protons, electrons, and molecules all in special and unique combinations. Everything and everyone was reducible to matter. History had no meaning or overriding purpose behind it. It was merely a series of events linked together by cause and effect. This was the worldview of naturalism.

While modern man believed in the goodness of knowledge and was optimistic about what his quest had the potential to do, the ultimate effect of naturalism was to take away man's dignity and purpose and leave him with no meaning. He was just another cog in the wheel. While man reasoned this way in his mind, his heart could not accept the implications and conclusions of such a philosophy. Man could not live without significance or meaning so he had to create meaning. This was done by dividing reality into two separate arenas; the objective and the subjective. Science ruled over the objective arena, but feelings and experience ruled over the subjective.

This had a profound effect on ethics and values. With the removal of God there was no longer any basis for establishing right and wrong. There were no more absolutes. Absolute truth in the arena of values gave way to situation ethics. The old values based upon revelation were destroyed, but man could "find no way to generate with certainty any new values. In the resulting vacuum the impoverished values of personal peace and affluence had come to stand supreme."[20]

A Comparison Between the Worldviews of Theism and Modernism		
	THEISM	MODERNISM
Center of the worldview	God	Man
Truth	Revealed by God — Scripture	Discovered by Scientific Method/Observation/ Rational Mind
God	Creator/Transcendant/ Immanent/Personal	Distant/Removed/ Unnecessary
Matter	Created by God	Eternal
Man	Created in the Image of God	Combination of Physical Elements
History	Purpose and Direction	Cause and Effect — but no Purpose or Direction
Ethics	Based on God's Character/ Revealed in Scripture/ Absolute	Situational/Personal

Life Application and Implication For Ministry

1. Have your students write out their worldview. Be sure that their worldview answers all of the basic questions concerning origins, life, epistemology, man, history, etc.

2. Think through how the different worldviews affect one's daily choices. Would you live any differently if you followed a different worldview? If so, how? Why?

3. Have your group make a list of all the ways that man is made "in the image of God." How does man exercise or reflect God's image in his day to day life? How does the modern worldview take away the dignity of man?

4. How does a worldview affect one's conclusions about such issues as abortion, euthanasia, suicide, history and ethics?

5. Modern man hoped that knowledge and science would provide the answers to man's problems. What destroyed that belief? Why?

Notes

1. William Mahedy and Janet Bernardi, *A Generation Alone*, 40.

2. Kevin Graham Ford, *Jesus For a New Generation*, 113.

3. David S. Dockery, ed., *The Challenge of Postmodernism: An Evangelical Engagement* (Wheaton, IL: Victor Books, 1995), 11.

4. James W. Sire, *The Universe Next Door: A Basic World View Catalog* (Downers Grove, IL: InterVarsity Press, 1976), 17-18.

5. Ibid., 25.

6. Ibid., 27.

7. Genesis 1:26-27.

8. Harold H. Titus and Marilyn S. Smith, *Living Issues In Philosophy* (New York: D. Van Nostrand Company, 1974), 23.

9. Berkhof, L., *Systematic Theology* (Grand Rapids: Eerdmans, 1939), 193.

10. Ibid., 204.

11. Psalm 8:3-8.

12. Sire, *The Universe Next Door*, 40.

13. Peter Medawar, "On 'The Effecting of All Things Possible,'" *The Listener*, 2 October 1969, 7, quoted in Sire.

14. Sire, *The Universe Next Door*, 64.

15. *Humanist Manifestos I and II* (Buffalo: Prometheus Books, 1973), 17. The *Humanist Manifesto II* is also published in *The Humanist* (September-October) 1973.

16. Ernest Becker, *The Denial of Death* (New York: The Free Press, 1973).

17. Ecclesiastes 3:11.

18. Sire, *The Universe Next Door*, 90.

19. Stanley J. Grenz, "Postmodernism and the Future of Evangelical Theology: Star Trek and the Next Generation," *Evangelical Review of Theology* 18 (October 1994), 324.

20. Francis A. Schaeffer, *How Should We Then Live?: The Rise and Decline of Western Thought and Culture* (Old Tappan, NJ: Fleming H. Revell, 1976), 209.

The Development of a Postmodern Worldview

A massive intellectual revolution is taking place that is perhaps as great as that which marked off the modern world from the Middle Ages. The foundations of the modern world are collapsing, and we are entering a postmodern world. — Diogenes Allen in *Christian Belief In A Postmodern World*[1]

We are experiencing enormous structural change in our country and in our world — change that promises to be greater than the invention of the printing press, greater than the Industrial Revolution, and greater than the rise and demise of communism. Our world is changing so quickly that we can barely keep track of what is happening, much less figure out how to respond. — Leith Anderson in *A Church For the Twenty-first Century*[2]

Generally perceived as positivistic, technocentric, and rationalistic, universal modernism has been identified with the belief in linear progress, absolute truths, the rational planning of ideal social orders, and the standardization of knowledge and production. Fragmentation, indeterminacy, and intense distrust of all universal or "totalizing" discourses (to use the favoured phrase) are the hallmark of postmodern thought. — David Harvey in *The Condition of Postmodernity*[3]

In the past, when one framework for knowledge was thought to be inadequate, it was replaced by another framework. The goal of postmodernism is to do without frameworks for knowledge altogether. . . Postmodernism is a worldview that denies all worldviews. — Gene Edward Veith, Jr. in *Postmodern Times: A Christian Guide to Contemporary Thought and Culture*[4]

Postmodernism is a new set of assumptions about reality, which goes far beyond mere relativism. It impacts our literature, our dress, our art, our architecture, our music, our sense of right and wrong, our self-identity, and our theology. Postmodernism tends to view human experience as incoherent, lacking absolutes in the area of truth and meaning. — David S. Dockery in *The Challenge of Postmodernism: An Evangelical Engagement*[5]

131

When reading through the latest literature on sociological and philosophical observations, it seems that most everyone is in agreement that we have left the worldview of modernity and have entered into a new era — that of the postmodern. While there is agreement that a worldview shift has taken place, there is less agreement on how to describe this new worldview. Most definitions seem to hold some issues in common, but there is a wide variety of opinions on the overall definition.

There are four fundamental values which make up the mindset of modernity. Postmodernism is a rejection or reaction to those fundamental views. The four fundamental values which depict the modern mindset are:

1) Moral relativism: This teaches that what is right is dictated by culture, social location and situation. The usual way this is presented is, "What is true for you is true for you, and what is true for me is true for me."

2) Autonomous individualism: This assumes that moral authority comes essentially from within. Ultimate moral authority is self-generated. In the end, we answer to no one but ourselves. Our choices are ours alone, determined by our personal pleasure, and not by any higher moral authority.

3) Narcissistic hedonism: This focuses on egocentric personal pleasure. The popular ethical expression of this mindset is simply this: "If it makes you happy, and it doesn't hurt anyone else, then it's 'okay.'"

4) Reductive naturalism: This reduces what is reliably known to what one can see, hear and empirically investigate. If it cannot be examined in a tangible, scientific manner, then it is not simply unknowable, it is meaningless.[6]

James Sire suggests five different aspects which he believes characterizes postmodernism. Notice how they differ from those of the worldview of modernity. They are:

1) Things and events do not have intrinsic meaning. There is only continuous interpretation of the world.

2) Continuous examination of the world requires a contextual

examination; we ourselves are a part of the context.

3) Interpretation depends not on the external text or its author, but on the relative viewpoint and particular values of the interpreter.

4) Language is not neutral, but relative and value-laden.

5) Language conveys ideology.[7]

Just when did this change take place, this movement from the modern to the postmodern? "The actual word 'postmodern' was first used by Federico de Onis in the 1930s within the arts to indicate a minor reaction to modernism."[8] Later it was used to describe a new style of architecture. But not until the 1970s did postmodernism gain widespread attention as a label for theories about language and culture that was being expounded in the English and philosophy departments in many universities. "It came to characterize a movement away from meta-narratives (or broad schemes of interpretation.) It called for a deconstruction of any perspective that claimed absolute authority of a particular viewpoint."[9] "Postmodernism is, in short, a reaction against the rationalism and scientism that dominated the Enlightenment and its legacy that we continue to live with in the twilight of the twentieth century."[10]

From a historical standpoint, modernity reigned from 1789 to 1989, from the Bastille to the fall of the Berlin Wall.[11] Modernity was characterized by the autonomous nature of the individual and his ability to construct a coherent whole to life through the use of the scientific method and rational thinking. The optimism of this period was based upon the belief that science and technological advances would bring about an end to the problems of man and usher in a new era characterized by global peace and prosperity.

In the premodern or theistic worldview, God was the center or focus of reality. In modernity, autonomous man is the center. Postmodernism is characterized by the belief that "there is no center, only plural possibilities of perspectives."[12]

The Star Trek Analogy

Stanley J. Grenz has come up with an simple way of illustrating and comparing the differences between modernity and the postmodern. He presents it in a way that is readily understood by Xers and Boomers alike. He compares the mission, crew, captain and heroes of the original *Star Trek* with that of *Star Trek: The Next Generation*. In the original *Star Trek*, the mission of the starship *Enterprise* was to "seek out new worlds, and to boldly go where no man has gone before." Notice that it centered on "man" — man the rugged individual, man the leader. In *The Next Generation*, the mission is "to go where no *one* has gone before." It is gender sensitive. It does not assume male leadership or dominance.

The purpose of the mission changes with the two shows. In the original the purpose was "to explore new worlds, to seek out new civilizations." But underneath that directive was the understanding that these new worlds and civilizations would be brought into the Federation. There is a sense of conquest. In the new show the crew of the *Enterprise* learn from alien cultures rather than just assimilating them. It represents a shift in worldview that supports the idea of pluralism. No one culture or its values are superior to another. Every culture can learn from the others and tolerance and respect are the desired values and virtues.

The crew is different with the two ships. In the original *Star Trek* the crew was comprised of various nationalities of people working together for the common benefit of all mankind. The message was obvious. We are all humans and we must learn to overcome our differences and join forces in order to complete our "quest for certain, objective knowledge of the entire universe."[13] The human crew of *The Next Generation* are joined by humanoid life forms from other parts of the universe. This underscores a basic assumption of postmodernism — man is not capable of completing his quest for knowledge alone. The individual cannot accomplish it by himself, he is dependent upon the universal community.

Captain Kirk is the hero in the original series. No matter what kind of galactic problem the ship and crew encountered, Kirk was usually the one who saved the day. This epitomized the autonomy of modern man. In *The Next Generation* Jean-Luc Picard is not the only hero. Every major character has his or her "day in the sun" so to speak. Problems are solved and disasters averted by the efforts of the whole crew, not just the heroics of one person. Once again, this underscores the need for community.

The "ideal" man in the original series was Spock (even though he was not "technically" a typical man because he was half human and half Vulcan). Spock represented the ideal because he was completely rational and without emotion (or at least with his emotions kept under perfect control). Time and time again his "dispassionate rationality provided the calculative key necessary to solve the problems encountered by the *Enterprise*."[14] This portrayed modernity's belief that the answer to all of life's problems could be solved through rational expertise. In *The Next Generation*, Data replaces Spock. In a sense Data is the perfect Spock, because he is the ultimate rational thinker — for he is not humanoid at all, he is an android — a subhuman machine. But ironically, what Spock tried to rid himself of (his emotions) in order to be the "ideal" man, Data is trying to gain so that he may know better what it truly means to "be human." This represents the postmodern emphasis upon feelings and experience. For the postmodern man, truth is not just that which can be objectively studied, but it is also that which is felt and experienced subjectively.

Along these same lines, *The Next Generation* has introduced a new crew member, Counselor Troi. Her specialty or contribution to the overall success of the mission of the Enterprise is her intuition. She has been gifted with the ability to perceive the hidden feelings of others. Once again, this is a direct attack on the belief of modernity that truth can only be discovered through reason and objective observation. The postmodern man believes that what a person intuitively feels about a situation is just as valid a criteria for truth as rational deduction and scientific observation.

The problems that the two crews encounter are different. In the original series, the problems confronted by the crew of the *Enterprise* were usually alien life forms, technical problems with the ship or some other physical phenomena that could be directly observed, studied and conquered. In *The Next Generation* the problems are not always of a physical nature, but may be some subjective experience or other kind of problem dealing with time and space which is not quantifiable.

The earlier *Star Trek* basically ignored spiritual questions concerning God and religious belief. Once again, this is a reflection of the modern mind. Truth was only that which could be seen, observed, measured or rationally deduced. God was systematically removed from the worldview of the modern man. In contrast to its earlier counterpart, *The Next Generation* includes the supernatural, embodied in the strange character of "Q." Q has supernatural powers and comes and goes in and out of the lives of the crew of the Enterprise without warning. But the character of Q is not like the picture of God presented in the Bible. While he does have some of the classic attributes of the divine, he is morally ambiguous "displaying both benevolence and a bent toward cynicism and self-gratification."[15] This is representative of the feelings of the postmodern man. He is open to the possibility of God, but he is not at all sure that God is going to be kind or benevolent in his relationship to man.

Deconstruction

Deconstruction is one of the main concepts of the postmodern worldview. Its roots are based in communication and literary criticism. Deconstructionists reject the basic, historically accepted rules concerning communication and understanding in language. They do not believe that words have objective content. They teach that meaning is not inherent in a text itself, but emerges only as the interpreter enters into dialogue with the text.[16] To dialogue with the text means that the words presented are not sufficient in themselves to communicate meaning. The reader must infuse his own experiences and values into the text. This implies that all knowledge is historically implicated. Nothing is known apart from its cultural setting. There are no culturally neutral facts. Therefore, the meaning of a text is dependent on the perspective of the one who enters into dialogue with it, so that there are as many interpretations of a text as there are readers.

The deconstructionist does not believe that there is an objective reality "out there" in the "real" world. Reality is only that which we create in our minds through language. Knowledge is not so much found as it is made. The words we use can take on different shades of meaning depending upon who is speaking, who is listening and the context in which it is spoken. Therefore, words do not have objective meanings. "To interpret the meaning of a given text is to impose meaning on it. To say 'This is what it means' is to misread it."[17]

Coinciding with this idea, is the belief that every interpretation is just as valid as the next, even if they are contradictory because there are no absolutes in any area, only personal experience. The meaning of the text is then dependent upon the reader, upon what the reader brings with him into the text. Reality is reduced to a matter of perspective. This means that there is no one meaning of the world, no transcendent center to reality as a whole, but only individual interpretations of it. "The same analysis that purports to show that works of literature can have no objective meaning can apply to everything else, including science, reason, and theology."[18]

Deconstruction has even found its way into contemporary biblical hermeneutics. No longer is biblical truth ascertained by using the tools of higher criticism and literary analysis to derive from the text historically accurate knowledge about the persons, events, and religious understandings of the people who produced the ancient texts. Biblical truth is discovered when the reader enters into dialogue with the text.

The focus of interest is not so much on what produced the biblical texts as on what the texts, when fully engaged, produce in the reader. Thus, the positivistic objectification of the text which resulted inexorably in the dilemma of the subject-object paradigm of understanding by analysis has begun to give way to a hermeneutical paradigm of understanding by participative dialogue. Interpretation, in other words, is not a matter either of dominating the text by method or of submitting to the text in servile fideism, but of entering into genuine dialogue with it as it stands. Through this dialogue reader and text are mutually transformed.[19]

Deconstructionists see language as a tool of society to create meaning. They also view society from a negative standpoint and assume that all societies are inherently oppressive. This has driven them to develop "a hermeneutics of suspicion." Truth is not found in what is being objectively presented in a text, but in what is *not* being said, or in what is hidden. The task of the reader or the interpreter is to "deconstruct" or "unmask" the text to find the true meaning which is hidden behind the words. Coming from this worldview, the deconstructionist considers *all* truth claims as suspect and treats them as a cover-up for those in power.

What is ultimate effect of such a methodology upon the biblical text? Scripture is placed at the mercy of culture, rather than Scripture critiquing and transforming culture. A good example of this is the October 1993 meeting of the "Jesus Seminar." The Jesus Seminar was a group comprised of about seventy scholars whose goal was to examine the Gospel text using the postmodern-deconstructionist methodology and reduce the text to the "authentic" sayings of Jesus. For those involved in this task, their own social location and cultural context was more important to the interpretive process than the social location of the biblical author and text.

Norman R. Gulley identifies twenty major assumptions of those involved in the Jesus Seminar which were either directly expressed by the participants or obvious from their presentations. In all of the assumptions, culture, as expressed in the social location of the reader, is given a place of higher authority than the written text itself. Those twenty observations are:

1. The biblical interpreter does not begin with the biblical text but with the reader. This is in contrast to the historical paradigm which begins with the history behind the text, and the literary paradigm that begins with the text itself.

2. The reader is unable to transcend his/her social location.

3. The various liberation theologies, whether racial or feminist, are more interested in their personal agenda for liberation than in what the biblical text says in its own location.

4. True objectivity is impossible. At best, only a relative objectivity is attainable, for objectivity is itself a human construct.

5. All exegesis is eisegesis.

6. Socio-analytical reading of Scripture finds in the text what is relevant to the reader in his or her cultural location, the rest is ignored.

7. Global or universal interpretation of biblical texts is impossible. There are only local meanings.

8. The reader gives the biblical text its meaning.

9. The reader must liberate Scripture before it liberates the reader.

10. Victims, or the colonized, repudiate biblical texts that are products of oppressors, or the colonizers.

11. All Scripture is patriarchal or andro-centric, male-dominated and, therefore, is repudiated by feminist liberation.

12. Scripture was culture originated and can be rejected by readers living in the different social location of modern culture.

13. Readers need to appropriate Scripture to their social location.

14. Revelation never ceases. It is present in preaching today.

15. There are no absolute statements in Scripture.

16. Certain biblical texts are offensive to readers in cultural locations where their practice is different from that given in Scripture, such as in polytheistic cultures.

17. Yet, the claim is also made that polytheism is taught in Scripture.

18. Pluralism is presented as true liberation beyond the narrower confines of Scripture.

19. Because of Scripture, the history of Christianity has been the most destructive religion in history.

20. Because of Scripture, missionaries have equated deculturization as christianization. So to become a Christian, an Indian, for example, had to renounce his Indian culture.[20]

When this approach was applied to specific biblical texts, the result was an interpretation based on one's national, tribal, or local perspective. It produced "a hopeless and complex pluralism. There was no one Word from God but a multiplex of cultural words from humans."[21]

Everything Is Relative

The postmodern mind views truth from a totally different perspective from that of the modern mind. In the modern worldview, truth is rational — it is objective, absolute and can be ascertained through human intellect and study. Postmodernists reject the idea that truth is rational and absolute. They believe that truth can be nonrational and even emotional and intuitive. For the postmodern man, truth is at best relative and possibly even nonexistent. Truth may just be a mental construct, something that man creates in his mind, but not something that "really exists" as a universal absolute. Since truth is no longer considered an absolute concept, it follows that there are many truths. There is your truth, my truth, his truth and her truth. No one truth is more valid than any other. It is even possible for these truths to be diametrically opposed to one another. The postmodern man sees no problem in believing that two opposing ideas can be held to be true at the same time. Xers are completely comfortable with paradox.

How did this shift from absolutes to relativity come about? It began with a new scientific paradigm. The modern worldview was grounded in Newtonian physics but this gave way to new ideas developed by Einstein's theory of relativity.

> In a Newtonian worldview it was possible to conceive of absolute contexts of space and time within which an object could be isolated. But with Einstein's development of relativity physics, common-sense notions of the absoluteness of space and time have been abandoned. It can no longer be taken for granted that measurements of either distance or duration in one frame of reference will be identical to those taken in another.[22]

The developments of quantum physics questioned the common-sense notion of a substantial universe. Quantum physics seems to imply that the universe at its most fundamental level, does not seem to be composed of stuff or things at all but rather of dynamic relations.

> As quantum theory has developed, it has become evident that certain characteristics are coupled in such a way that to determine one characteristic is to disable one from determining the other. Werner Heisenberg expressed this finding in his principle of uncertainty. It seems that at the core of reality there is an uncertainty (or indeterminacy) which no amount or quality of observation can overcome.[23]

All of this has combined to present a different picture of reality and life. The world can no longer be viewed as a system of independent atomic parts linked together by external mechanical relations, but, instead, as a dynamic nexus of internal relatings, actual and potential. There can be no observation in which the object observed and person observing are absolutely separate and independent from one another. In other words, there are no facts or truths in nature which exist independently from the observer. There is a dynamic relationship in which meaning or truth is the combination of the interaction between the object and the observer. "All knowers are participants in that which is to be known."[24]

What are the implications of Einstein's theory of relativity as it is lived out in society? 1) There is no such thing as an objective point of view in matters of physics; all viewpoints are relative in time and space. 2) Under some conditions, subjective experience supersedes objective measurements. 3) Space and time are relative, not absolute, concepts and depend on such factors as relative motion and the point of view of the observer.[25] If these are true for the realm of physics, then the postmodern mind also transfers these assumptions to the areas of ethics, morality, philosophy, and religion. This means that there can be no absolute, objective point of view in matters of morality and religion, only situational ethics. A typical response from an Xer might be, "You have your truth, and I have mine."

This has affected how decisions concerning morality are determined. It used to be, under the theistic worldview, that morality was objectively based in the character of God as revealed in the Bible. During the modern era it moved to man as the center and was based upon what was best for society. In the postmodern worldview the new basis for determining morality has shifted from outside of man to inside him. Personal feelings and experience govern the new morality. This evolution of morality didn't take place all at once, but is the result of the gradual movement away from biblical morality. Fran Sciacca presents an excellent chart which maps out this moral deterioration in the life of American teenagers.[26]

MORAL STANDARDS		
IDEOLOGY	TIME	BELIEF
Biblical Morality	1800-early 1900s	"Certain things are right and wrong, and I know why."
Abiblical Morality	1900s-1950s	"Certain things are right and wrong, but I don't know why."
Immorality	1960-early 1970s	"Certain things are right and wrong, but I don't care!"
Amorality	late 1900s	"There's no such thing as right and wrong!"
		Source: *Generation At Risk*

The implications of Einstein's theory of relativity also means for the postmodern mind that subjective experience may supersede logic and objective facts. Since there is no absolute truth or morality, a person is free to believe and choose what makes him "feel good." Xers are not as concerned about facts as they are experience. Therefore, they place a higher priority on relationships and experiences that make them feel good, than pursuing intellectual questions about what constitutes truth. Feelings and relationships are what matter, not dispassionate knowledge and logical arguments.

Xers are often accused of being "slackers" because they won't take a stand on an issue. It is not that they are intellectually lazy or don't have strong opinions, but if there is no absolute truth, if all opinions are equally valid, then what is the purpose of arguing or debating an issue?

If all truth claims are relative, then any claims about deity are also up for grabs. You believe in your God and I believe in mine. Anything that smacks of exclusiveness, such as John 14:6 or Acts 4:12, is highly suspect to the postmodern mind. Religious pluralism is the result.

What does all of this mean to a typical Xer growing up in this environment? How does it affect him as this philosophy trickles down through society? If you grow up in a godless, mindless universe where there are no rules, no right, no wrong, no meaning and no absolute truth, then the best that you can do is just "survive." That is why pragmatism is one of their chief characteristics — does it work? They don't need, or even want, to know why. They don't require any justification for something because in a relative worldview, everything and every belief is justifiable from some standpoint. The bottom line is simply "will this work in my life?"

What Are the Implications For the Church?

I want to say up front that not everything about postmodernism is bad, even though it may seem at first that it rejects about everything that Christianity is based upon. There are some hopeful aspects to the postmodern worldview in ways that were not present in the worldview of modernity. It provides a window of opportunity for the church to reach out and present the hope of the gospel. But if the church is to reach the postmodern generation, it will not do it with the same old methods. A new apologetic and a new way of doing evangelism is needed so that the life-changing power of the unchanging gospel can break through the chaos and hopelessness of this next generation. The church needs to be aware of the strategies and methods that will be effective in communicating the gospel to the postmodern mind.

The first bridge to cross in reaching out to the postmodern man is to join in and affirm their abandonment of the rationalist belief system as the *only* source of truth. The postmodern worldview allows for the existence of realities that science cannot measure — thus opening up the possibility for the supernatural and the spiritual. The collapse of the modern worldview has given the Christian a beachhead in which to present the mystery of God, for God himself is beyond the capacity of reason to fully fathom. In Isaiah 55:9 God says, "As the heavens are higher than the earth, so are my ways higher than your ways and my thoughts than your thoughts." This is a declaration that one cannot know everything about God through human reason. There are realities that go beyond it.

The modern worldview elevated man as the center of reality. The rugged individual who faced and conquered all the problems that life presented through his own effort and education was the model. But this ended up promoting an egocentric man who was only concerned about what happened to himself — having his own needs met. He exploited others and the environment in order to satisfy his personal desires.

The postmodern man views himself as a part of a larger whole — he sees a need to be a responsible member of a global community. The book of Acts presents the Christian faith as a religion that is to be lived out in the context of a healing, caring and supportive community (Acts 2:42-47; 4:32-35).

Modern man set out to discover all of the inner workings and wonders of nature in order to control it and make his life more comfortable. While many of the scientific discoveries did benefit man in the areas of medicine and technology, there were also some serious negative consequences as a byproduct of the industrial age. Pollution threatened the drinking water and the habitats of some forms of wildlife were threatened. Millions of acres of rain forest were cleared in the name of "progress." Natural resources were consumed as if they were unlimited.

The postmodern worldview teaches a more responsible attitude towards the environment. Xers are much more ecologically minded and seek to live in harmony with nature instead of exploiting and conquering it. The Christian seeks to walk a balance between these two views. In the garden of Eden, man was given the mandate by God to "fill the earth and subdue it" (Gen 1:28). But he was also supposed to be a responsible steward of God's creation. He was not to be abusive or exploit the earth.

The modern man rejected God because he could not be confirmed through the laws governing the scientific method. Postmodern man does not place a high degree of confidence in scientific laws or trust in mental gymnastics, but seeks out relationships and desires to live in community. Christians need to help Xers understand that Christianity is not a set of rules and regulations, but a personal relationship with the living God.

Modern man ended up in existential despair. When God was removed from his worldview, the ground for man's uniqueness and significance was taken away. He was reduced to simply being a chance combination of material elements. There was no overriding purpose for history or any hope to transcend his finite condition. He started out optimistic but ended up pessimistic. Christianity offers a ground for hope and meaning once again.

While postmodernism does intersect with Christianity at

some important junctures, one should be careful not to give the impression that a Christian can accept and live comfortably with all of the tenets of postmodern philosophy. The Christian believes that the Bible presents absolute truth in the realm of morals and spirituality — it is not relative. God is the center and focus of the universe and only through his Son can man be redeemed. There is no place for religious pluralism.

While the Christian must never compromise the essence of the gospel story, he should be open to new ways of communicating it, especially in the postmodern world. The good news is that narrative or story telling is one of the most effective ways to reach the postmodern mind. Everyone has "their own story" — their pilgrimage through the pitfalls and trials of life. Xers love to tell their story and have others listen and care about what they have struggled through. Listening to others tell their story is an effective means of opening doors of opportunity to share "the old, old story, of Jesus and his love." The story of Jesus' love transcends all cultures and time periods with its message of healing love, forgiveness and reconciliation.

Life Application and Implication For Ministry

1. Look through the differences between the basic tenets of modernism as compared with that of postmodernism. Do the members of your youth group or Sunday School class exhibit a modern or postmodern view? How would this affect your lesson preparation? What teaching methods are going to be the most persuasive for the modern mind? What teaching methods are going to be the most effective with the postmodern mind?

2. Challenge your youth group or Sunday School class to list as many differences or similarities as they can find between *Star Trek* and *The New Generation*. Use the insights of Stanley Grenz as your model. Make application to the world your teens live in. Which one do they like the best? Understand the best? Most comfortable with?

3. Have your group brainstorm and come up with as many situations as they can think of where the context is going to affect the meaning of a message. Can they think of any situations where the context would not make any difference? How does this affect how we teach biblical exegesis? Think through the implications of a timeless, unchanging message, but application in a variety of settings and cultures.

4. The postmodern mind has no problem believing that two contradictory ideas can be held as truthful at the same time because there is no absolute truth. The Bible contains many paradoxes, e.g., you must lose your life in order to find it; the one who serves becomes the greatest of all, etc. How would you explain the difference between two contradictory truths and paradox?

Notes

1. Diogenes Allen, *Christian Belief In A Postmodern World* (Louisville: John Knox Press, 1989), 2.

2. Leith Anderson in *A Church For the Twenty-first Century* (Minneapolis: Bethany House, 1992), 17.

3. David Harvey, *The Condition of Postmodernity* (Cambridge, MA: Basil Blackwell, 1989), 9.

4. Gene Edward Veith, Jr., *Postmodern Times: A Christian Guide to Contemporary Thought and Culture* (Wheaton, IL: Crossway Books, 1994), 49.

5. David S. Dockery, ed., *The Challenge of Postmodernism*, 14.

6. Thomas Oden, "Back to the Fathers," interview by Christopher Hall, *Christianity Today*, 24 September 1990, 28-31. See also: Thomas C. Oden, *Two Worlds: Notes On the Death of Modernity in America & Russia* (Downers Grove, IL: InterVarsity Press, 1992), 33-36, and James Emery White, "Evangelism in a Postmodern World," in David S. Dockery, ed., *The Challenge of Postmodernism*, 362-363.

7. James Sire, "Logocentricity and Postmodern Apologetic: On Being a Fool for Christ and an Idiot for Nobody" (Unpublished paper presented at the Wheaton Theology Conference, 7-8 April 1994), quoted in Dockery, *The Challenge of Postmodernism*, 14.

8. Craig Van Gelder, "Postmodernism As An Emerging Worldview," *Calvin Theological Journal*, 26 1991, 412.

9. Ibid., 413.

10. Mark S. McLeod, "Making God Dance: Postmodern Theorizing and the Christian College," *Christian Scholar's Review*, 21 March 1992, 279.

11. Dockery, *The Challenge of Postmodernism*, 20.

12. Van Gelder, "Postmodernism," 415.

13. Stanley J. Grenz, "Postmodernism and the Future of Evangelical Theology: Star Trek and the Next Generation," *Evangelical Review of Theology*, 18 October 1994, 325.

14. Ibid.

15. Ibid., 329.

16. Ibid., 326.

17. Kevin Graham Ford, *Jesus For a New Generation*, 120.

18. Veith, *Postmodern Times*, 51.

19. Sandra M. Schneiders, "Does the Bible Have a Postmodern Message?" in *Postmodern Theology: Christian Faith in a Pluralist World*, ed. Frederic B. Burnham (New York: Harper & Row, 1989), 61-62.

20. Normal R. Gulley, "Reader-Response Theories in Postmodern Hermeneutics: A Challenge to Evangelical Theology," in David S. Dockery, ed., *The Challenge of Postmodernism*, 220-221.

21. Ibid., 222.

22. James B. Miller, "The Emerging Postmodern World," in *Postmodern Theology: Christian Faith in a Pluralist World*, ed. Frederic B. Burnham, 9.

23. Ibid., 9-10.

24. Ibid., 10.

25. Ford, *Jesus For a New Generation*, 114.

26. Fran Sciacca, *Generation at Risk: What Legacy Are the Baby-Boomers Leaving Their Kids?* (Chicago: Moody Press, 1990), 117.

SECTION 3

Understanding and Meeting the Needs of Generation X

Comparing Two Worlds

Even when I am old and gray, do not forsake me, O God, till I declare your power to the next generation, your might to all who are to come. — Psalm 71:18

O my people, hear my teaching; listen to the words of my mouth. I will open my mouth in parables, I will utter hidden things, things from of old — what we have heard and known what our fathers have told us. We will not hide them from their children; we will tell the next generation the praiseworthy deeds of the Lord, his power, and the wonders he has done. — Psalm 78:1-4

Has anything like this ever happened in your days or in the days of your forefathers? Tell it to your children and let your children tell it to their children and their children to the next generation. — Joel 1:2b-3

The social regression of the last 30 years is due in large part to the enfeebled state of our social institutions and their failure to carry out a critical and time-honored task: the moral education of the young. We desperately need to recover a sense of the fundamental purpose of education, which is to engage in the architecture of souls. When a self-governing society ignores this responsibility, then . . . it does so at its peril. — William J. Bennett in *The Index of Leading Cultural Indicators*[1]

The real crisis is one of character. Today's high school seniors live in a world of misplaced values. They have no sense of discipline. No goals. They care only for themselves. In short, they are becoming a generation of undisciplined cultural barbarians. — Barbara Walters in a 1988 television special on education titled *America's Kids, Why They Flunk*[2]

It has been said that the one who fails to study history is doomed to repeat it. So it is with Generation X. Although there are some unique situations and new problems that Generation X has had to face on their own, many of the essential issues have been problems that have plagued other generations in other cultures and time periods. I am indebted to Mark Scott, Professor of Homiletics at Ozark Christian College, for pointing out some fascinating parallels between the problems of postexilic Israel and Generation X. If we can get a handle on how Israel responded to the great cultural shift and generational problems in the days following the Babylonian captivity, perhaps we may find some useful insights in reaching Generation X in our time.

A Loss of Center

For the Hebrew people God was center of their culture. Their society was formed around a Theocracy, a covenantal relationship with Jehovah God. The conditions and stipulations concerning this covenant were set down in the Law that Moses received on top of Mt. Sinai. More than 600 rules were given which were to govern their daily transactions in business and to regulate their social and spiritual life. Worship, holidays, daily and weekly sacrifices took place at the temple. In fact, the temple was the only place were sacrifices could be legally offered. So the temple became the center of their society. It represented God's presence to them. Three of the Jewish holidays required all males to travel to Jerusalem to make their sacrifices and to participate in the worship rituals at the temple.

But soon after the death of Solomon and the beginning of the divided kingdom the temple began to lose its significance and its important place in the daily life of the Israelites. Jeroboam, the king of the ten northern tribes of Israel, feared what might happen if the Israelites went back to Jerusalem to worship. To keep the people from returning to the temple and reestablishing their previous loyalties to the house of David, Jeroboam had two golden calf idols set up to worship. He placed one in Dan and the other in Bethel, the northern and southern edges of his kingdom. He installed his own priests and instituted his own religious festivals to take the place of those in Jerusalem at the temple.[3]

What Jeroboam did was pure idolatry. It went against the very core of the law and the covenant relationship with God. What was the result of this action? Ultimately it led to the downfall of the capital city of Samaria and the Assyrian captivity of the ten northern tribes. "They rejected his decrees and the covenant he had made with their fathers and the warnings he had given them. They followed worthless idols and themselves became worthless" (2 Kings 17:15). The ten northern tribes of Israel were carried away into captivity, never to return. Their society and culture collapsed because of the loss of center — their rejection of God, the law and the temple. It was a blow from which they never recovered.

Rather than learning a lesson from her northern sister, the southern tribe of Judah followed the idolatrous ways of Israel and the surrounding heathen nations. King Ahaz removed portions of the temple and even had a pagan altar from Damascus copied and set up in the temple.[4] Manasseh built altars to all the starry hosts in the temple and immersed himself in the practices of the occult and pagan worship. He defiled the temple of God by placing an Asherah pole in the midst of it.[5] God punished Judah by allowing them to be taken into Babylonian captivity for seventy years. Sacrifice ceased during this time period because the temple in Jerusalem was destroyed by Nebuchadnezzar and it was not lawful for the people to offer sacrifices anywhere else. Even if they had wanted to, there was no legitimate place to offer sacrifice in the land of captivity.

Because of the need for a center, something to rally the people around and give them some sense of unity, the synagogues came into being during the time of the captivity and the study of the law became the focal point. It was recognized by the elders and leaders in Israel that the people needed a central focus, some common vision or concern which would give them a sense of shared purpose and heritage as a people once again.

That was Israel. Now let's look at our present situation. For seventeen centuries God was the center of Western Christian Civilization. Law and morality was based upon the revelation of

153

God as found in the Bible. Then came "The Enlightenment." God was removed from the focus and man took center stage. Reason and scientific discovery were held up as the salvation of all mankind. It was believed that science and reason would find a solution for all of the ills of mankind and usher man into a new age of utopia where there was no more sickness, no more ignorance, and no more wars.

But with the loss of God came a loss of meaning. Man was no longer unique, but just a combination of physical elements. History no longer had an overriding purpose or goal, but was simply the connection of a series of events linked only by cause and effect. Eventually, in the postmodern world, even cause and effect was destroyed because it was argued that the relationship between cause and effect was not *really* there, but was simply a construct of the human mind.

Morality lost its center because it used to be grounded in the character of God. When God was removed so was the basis for morality. There could be no more absolute truths because the ground upon which they were based was removed. Morality became utilitarian, what was best for society as a whole, or situational, what was best for the individual in that particular situation. This change has resulted in an increase in sexual promiscuity, fragmented families, selfishness and greed in the workplace and rampant crime.

A loss of center is also seen on a national level. America was founded by people who were in search of religious freedom. The great American statesman Patrick Henry said, "It cannot be emphasized too strongly or too often that this great nation was founded, not to be religionist but by Christians, not on religions but on the gospel of Jesus Christ."[6] The early founders based the Constitution and other early government documents upon the morals and values contained in Scripture. John Adams, our second president, said, "Our Constitution was made only for a moral and religious people. It is wholly inadequate for the government of any other."[7] James Madison, fourth president of the United States, agreed with this principle. He said, "The belief in a God All Powerful, wise and good, is essential to the moral order of the world and to the happiness of man."[8] Noah Webster echoed these same thoughts. He claimed:

> The religion which has introduced civil liberty, is the religion of Christ and his apostles, which enjoins humility, piety, and benevolence; which acknowledges in every person a brother, or a sister, and a citizen with equal rights. This is the genuine Christianity, and to this (Christianity) we owe our free constitution of government.[9]

Today, instead of basing our laws and culture upon the knowledge of God and Scripture, our government has turned its back on its religious heritage. In 1947, the U.S. Supreme Court ignored 175 years of historically consistent rulings concerning religious involvement and the government and declared that there must be a separation between church and state.

What has been the result of this separation? One can almost chart to the day that as soon as prayer, the Bible and religion were taken out of our public schools and civil government, the moral character of our nation began to drop. This is evidenced in the rise in crime, pregnancies outside of wedlock, drug addiction and abuse. At the same time scholastic achievement began to fall. But this should come as no surprise because the great statesman Daniel Webster predicted it. He said:

> If we and our posterity neglect religious instruction and authority, violate the rules of eternal justice, trifle with the injunctions of morality . . . no man can tell how sudden a catastrophe may overwhelm us that shall bury all our glory in profound obscurity.[10]

If there is going to be any hope for our nation to survive, there must be revival. Only with a return to our center can there be any real hope of healing. If we cannot return to our religious roots, then destruction is inevitable.

> In terms of human history, religion is older than governments. There is no record anywhere, at any time, of any human society

without a religion. There is, similarly, no great civilization that has ever arisen without a religion — and no great civilization that has ever outlasted the loss of its religion.[11]

Biblical Illiteracy

Because of Israel's rejection of the covenant and her pursuit of idolatry, she did not teach the succeeding generations to honor and uphold the Mosaic law. In fact, after the return from Babylon, many of the Israelite children did not even know how to speak native Hebrew, let alone have a working knowledge of the law and its requirements. "Moreover, in those days I saw men of Judah who had married women from Ashdod, Ammon and Moab. Half of their children spoke the language of Ashdod or the language of one of the other peoples, and did not know how to speak the language of Judah."[12]

Since taking prayer and Bible reading out of the public schools the American people have become incredibly ignorant concerning biblical facts. Truly it can be said that willful ignorance in one generation produces true ignorance in the next. Since rejecting prayer and Bible study as legitimate activities for the public school, most American children don't even understand the basic divisions of Old and New Testaments, let alone the order of the individual books or the major people and doctrines contained in them. In a 1988 survey by The Gallup Organization, it was found that only 35% of the youth surveyed could name the four Gospels and only 66% knew the number of Jesus' disciples.[13] Only 9% of those same youth polled read the Bible daily, 10% read it two or three times a week, and 20% would read at least once a week.[14]

The most telling information concerning the crisis created by our biblical illiteracy and loss of center is seen in the loss of influence that religious instruction and training has had upon the daily lives of teens in America. Eighty-seven percent of teens indicate that friends have a great deal of influence upon their lives, home has 51%, school 45%, music 41%, television

32%, movies 19% and religion only 13%.[15] When asked how interested they were in subjects such as the Bible, church, God and Jesus Christ, only 23% indicated that they were very interested, while 53% were somewhat interested.[16] Along with a return to God, our youth need to be reacquainted with the Word of God and how it can make an impact upon their lives.

Family Fragmentation

One of the results of living in the foreign land of Babylon was the intermarriage of many of the Israelites with the various Gentile neighbors surrounding them. This was strictly forbidden by the Mosaic law.[17] Yet, in the return to Jerusalem and the ensuing resettling of the city, it was found that many of the people of Israel, including the priests and the Levites, had not kept themselves pure but had taken foreign wives. Ezra's solution to the problem was to command all of those who had married foreign wives to separate themselves from them and send them away — divorce.

"The number of divorces in America has increased by nearly 200 percent in the last 30 years, while today, the percentage of people marrying is at an all-time low."[18] This increase in divorce has also led to an increase in the number of children who are directly affected by divorce. "Less than 60 percent of all children today are living with their biological, married parents."[19]

Secularization of the People of God

When Israel abandoned Jehovah God and the temple as her center, she substituted the pagan worship of the gods and goddesses of the heathen nations around her. The people involved themselves in occult practices, astrology, the sacrifice of their children to Molech and other despicable idolatrous acts.[20]

The displaced people who were deported from their native lands and resettled in the towns of Samaria practiced a type of syncretism. It was true that they worshipped Jehovah God, "but they also served their own gods in accordance with the customs of the nations from which they had been brought."[21] When the first exiles of Babylon returned to Jerusalem and began to restore the temple, the people who had remained in Samaria wanted to help with the rebuilding of the temple, but they were not allowed to have a part in its reconstruction because they did not worship Jehovah God only, but had also included the gods of the foreign people who had settled around them. This eventually developed into the "Samaritan problem" of the New Testament. It all started because they were too inclusive in their worship and did not worship God alone.

So it is with Generation X. They are very religious, very interested in spiritual things, but it would be a grave error to interpret that spiritual hunger and interest as "Christian." The religious interests and practices of Generation X are very syncretistic. A typical Xer will borrow a little bit of ritual from Catholicism, some meditation techniques from Eastern mysticism, some native American practices and wrap them all up in a New Age philosophy and make that his own special brand of "spirituality."

Legalism On Horizon to Protect Perimeters

As was previously mentioned, when the Israelites lost their center, the temple and all its accompanying rituals, they had to have something take its place. They needed something that would act as a glue that would hold their culture together and give them some kind of an identity. With all of the changes and chaos that came with the Babylonian captivity, they needed something that would give them some stability and help to settle them in the midst of all the changes that were taking place.

The study of the law is what developed. Synagogues became the gathering place for the leaders in Jewish society. At the synagogue, the leaders would discuss every possible life situation and think through every variation of as many issues pertaining to the law as they could. Out of these discussions and times of study came the Talmud, or the oral interpretation of the law. Eventually, these interpretations were looked upon as being just as binding as the law itself. The religious group known as the Pharisees grew out of these studies.

The Pharisees had a great desire to protect the law and its oral interpretation. However, in their devotion to the law and its interpretation, they went to such an extreme that they became fanatic legalists. In the New Testament, Jesus accused them of nullifying the word of God by their traditions.[22]

Just as the Jews were trying to hold on to their identity by devotion to the law, so it is that there is a portion of conservative Christianity which has responded to the chaotic changes taking place in society by manifesting a legalistic adherence to many traditional methods and programs found in the church. These people decry the introduction of such things as praise choruses and singing from an overhead as a departure from the faith. The correct way to sing songs of worship to God is from the hymnbook! These are the same people who get upset when a teenager (Generation X) wears a cap into the sanctuary for worship service and doesn't take it off. It is not that any of these issues are inherently important, but they represent some of the changes which are taking place in society around them which deeply affect their lives, but which they have no control over. So, the few things that they do have some control over, they are fanatically dedicated to preserving.

The problem is that they have equated tradition with the word of God. If the church allows herself to get stuck in a legalistic battle over form and tradition, she may miss an opportunity to reach an entire generation. Generation X is very comfortable with change. They like to do things differently — their way. If the church is to reach Generation X, she must be open to new possibilities for worship and evangelism.

Religion of Form — Little Substance

Closely tied to the problem of legalism, is the danger of reducing a relationship with God to merely adherence to particular rituals. It all becomes a matter of outward form instead of being inward transformation. The Pharisees were concerned about ritual cleansing, tithing every last seed from their garden, but neglected the weightier matters of the law — justice and mercy and faithfulness.[23]

The church can end up making this same mistake if it gets hung up on traditional modes of worship, times of services or what constitutes acceptable apparel to be worn to services. Generation X is very scornful of any attempt to make them conform to any outward standards. They are not as concerned about outward appearances as much as they are concerned about inward experiences.

Another danger of a religion of form is that it has the tendency to produce short-term commitment. As long as you looked right in your coat and tie or hat and dress and bowed your head when the elder prayed, put in your offering when the plate was passed, and partook of communion then you have fulfilled your spiritual obligation for the week.

True Christianity is much more than that. It transforms one's entire life from the inside out. When Jesus Christ reigns over one's heart everything is changed. It is a life that flows out of a dynamic relationship with the living Lord. It can never be reduced to mere form. It must be a personal experience, not conformance to an outward ritual.

Neglect of Personal Holiness and Piety

The prophet Jeremiah brought this charge against Israel: "Are they ashamed of their loathsome conduct? No, they have no shame at all; they do not even know how to blush."[24] Israel had allowed herself to be seduced by the immorality of the Canaanites which was part and parcel of the worship of Baal and Asherah. When the problem was pointed out to them by the prophet, the people refused to acknowledge the seriousness of it. "They dress the wound of my people as though it were not serious. 'Peace, peace,' they say, when there is no peace."[25]

The concept of holiness is all but removed from our postmodern culture. With the abandonment of moral absolutes, anything goes. Sexual immorality is rampant. Cheating is common and drug abuse is at epidemic proportions. Crime is becoming an ever increasing problem among youth. There is no personal accountability, no standards that are held up for all people to follow. It is only the personal pursuit of pleasure. If a teenager should take a stand for morality or holiness publicly in school, more likely than not they would be ridiculed by their teacher and peers for even suggesting that there is a certain way which we *ought* to live and behave. Yet, if our culture is to survive, we must raise up young people who are willing to take a stand for personal holiness and piety or all of our social and moral foundations will collapse.

Stress Level High Over Lack of Control Over One's Destiny

One of the major issues which brought a great deal of stress into the lives of the Jews during the captivity was their loss of control over their own destiny. They had not chosen to live in Babylon — they had been forcibly deported by King Nebuchadnezzar. Psalm 137 tells of the captives' grief and their longing to go back to their homeland. "By the rivers of Babylon we sat and wept when we remembered Zion."[26] Their grief and stress was over the circumstances in which they found themselves and they were unable to do anything about it. They were a conquered people. They had to submit to the powers that were over them until the time of their captivity was fulfilled and God would move in the heart of a foreign king to allow the Israelites to return to their homeland.

So it is with Generation X. They find themselves unwanted,

underemployed, poorly educated and without a very bright future ahead of them. They see the national debt continuing to grow at a monstrous rate. The burden of having to provide for the needs of all of the previous generations weighs heavily upon them. The demands on Social Security continue to escalate as the number of retirees grows, but the number of Xers who have decent paying jobs is very low. In order to make up the difference, they have to put in much more individually than did previous generations. This frustrates them and fills them with bitterness and resentment. They feel that they have been forced to pick up the tab for the carelessness and selfishness of previous generations. They are not sure that the jobs and resources needed will be there for them and the result is increased stress in their already stressed-out lives.

Conclusion

The circumstances that precipitated the crisis of the captivity and the postexilic period were different from those which brought about the postmodern worldview and the development of Generation X. Idolatry and the captivity brought about the crisis for the Jewish nation, whereas the enlightenment and the shift away from a theistic worldview brought about the existential crisis of the postmodern age. However, the parallels between them are certainly fascinating and merit our study. Certainly we must pay attention to the historical developments which followed Israel's loss of center and make application to our present situation where it is applicable. The fate of the next generation may depend upon it.

Life Application and Implication For Ministry

1. What are some other parallels that you find between post-exilic Israel and our present situation?
2. How can we regain the loss of our center? What is going to be the most practical and the most realistic? Campaign to

have prayer and Bible study returned to the public schools? Pull our children out of the public schools and place them in private Christian schools or home school?

3. Just as a nation can lose its center, so can a church or youth group. What should be the center of focus of a church? A youth group? How do you determine what the center should be? How can you tell if you are still on target or if you have lost your center?

4. What are you doing to ensure that you are not raising an entire generation of Biblical illiterates? How well do your people *really* know their Bible?

5. With the increase in the number of divorces, what is your church doing to strengthen families? (Check all that apply)
   ___ Nothing but I know that we should be doing something.
   ___ Showing various video series on related family issues.
   ___ Providing special classes on parenting.
   ___ Offering marriage enrichment retreats at least once a year.
   ___ Providing Christian counseling for families in crisis.

6. What is being done to promote personal holiness and commitment? Does your church promote:
   ___ Journaling   ___ Fasting   ___ Prayer
   ___ Meditation   ___ Bible Study ___ Service Projects
   ___ Memorization

Notes

1. William J. Bennett, *The Index of Leading Cultural Indicators* (Empower America, The Heritage Foundation & Free Congress Foundation) Vol 1 (March 1993), iii.

2. Barbara Walters, "America's Kids, Why They Flunk," a television special, quoted in Tim & Beverly LaHaye, *A Nation Without A Conscience* (Wheaton, IL: Tyndale House Publishers, 1994), 19.

3. See: 1 Kings 12:26-33.

4. See: 2 Kings 16:10-18.

5. See: 2 Kings 21:1-9.

6. Charles Barton, *The Myth of Separation* (Aledo, TX: WallBuilder Press, 1991), 25, quoted in David T. Moore, *Five Lies of the Century* (Wheaton, IL: Tyndale House Publishers, 1995),16.

7. Chuck Colson, Kingdoms in Conflict (Grand Rapids, MI: Zondervan, 1989), 47.

8. A.D. Wainwright, *Madison and Witherspoon: Theological Roots of American Political Thought*, 125, quoted in David T. Moore, *Five Lies of the Century*, 4.

9. Noah Webster, *The History of the United States* (New Haven, CT: Durrie & Peck, 1832), 300, quoted in David T. Moore, *Five Lies of the Century*,17.

10. Don Feder, "Independence Day: A Nation in Historical Denial," *Orange County Register*, 4 July 1993, quoted in David T. Moore, *Five Lies of the Century*, 5.

11. Otto Scott, "Psychiatry Discovers Religion," Chalcedon Report, no. 345 (April 1994), 3, quoted in Tim & Beverly LaHaye, *A Nation Without A Conscience*, 22.

12. Nehemiah 13:23-24.

13. Robert Bezilla, ed., *America's Youth 1977-1988* (Princeton, NJ: The Gallup Organization, 1988), 141.

14. Ibid., 143.

15. Robert Bezilla, ed., *America's Youth in the 1990s* (Princeton, NJ: The George H. Gallup International Institute, 1993), 30.

16. George Barna, *Today's Teens: A Generation in Transition* (Glendale, CA: Barna Research Group, 1991), 34-35.

17. See: Exodus 34:16 & Deuteronomy 7:3-4.

18. Bennett, *The Index*, 13.

19. U.S. Department of Commerce, Bureau of the Census, Current Population Reports, P-23, No. 180, "Marriage, Divorce and Remarriage in the 1990's," cited in William J. Bennett, *The Index*, 14.

20. 2 Kings 21:2-6.

21. 2 Kings 17:33.

22. Matthew 15:6.

23. Matthew 23:23.

24. Jeremiah 6:15.

25. Jeremiah 8:11.

26. Psalm 137:1.

Gateways to the Soul of Generation X

... And I wonder if this irony is the price we paid for the loss of God. But then I must remind myself we are living creatures — we have religious impulses — we must — and yet into what cracks do these impulses flow in a world without religion? It is something I think about every day. Sometimes I think it is the only thing I should be thinking about. — Douglas Coupland in *Life After God*[1]

"We don't want no frills, no dog-and pony show, no dancing-girls gospel," says twentysomething Piper Lowell, a Christian in the Washington, D.C., area. "What we want is unity, love and acceptance." — Andres Tapia in "Reaching The First Post-Christian Generation"[2]

Practically, for the church to welcome me it needs to honor the truth I bring with me, welcome my energy, and bless my inexperience. For me, there is nothing more discouraging and soul-sucking than entering a church and leaving without anyone saying hello, showing interest in me, or inviting me to be involved. — Jarrett Kerbel in "Generation's Faith"[3]

I had no mentors in the faith. There are no Christians within climbing distance on my family tree. When I came to God, I came out of desperation. — Piper Lowell in "Generation's Faith"[4]

Generation X is a disillusioned generation. There is a sense of hopelessness that pervades their lives. It is heard in their music[5] and seen in the way they dress. (You may have noticed that they have a preference for all black.) Xers feel abandoned and disconnected. They lack heroes and do not feel very optimistic about their future. They are void of any roots. If you will listen to their conversations you will find that they are angry; angry over what they feel should have rightly been theirs but was selfishly taken away from them by previous generations.[6]

They also feel cheated; cheated out of the kind of family life that they so desperately need and desire.

Because they have been so hurt they often come across as hard and uncaring. But don't let their tough exterior fool you. It is more a self-defense and survival technique than a true representation of what is inside. Underneath the hard facade is a heart that is lonely and crying out for someone to care.

Older generations see their rough exterior and bizarre dress (nose rings & body tattoos) and find them repugnant. Consequently, they either avoid any interaction with them or they come across as judgmental and harsh because of their criticisms of Xers' choice of hair styles, dress and jewelry.

What Xers don't need is more criticism and rejection. They have lived their whole lives with a sense of failure and disappointment. Bridges need to be built between the generations and healing administered to fragile and broken lives. Generation X is not going to respond to new arguments about the truth claims of Christianity. They are going to respond when they experience the genuine care, concern and involvement of Christian people reaching out in compassion and understanding.

> But my generation demands a different apologetic — an embodied apologetic, a flesh-and-blood apologetic, living and breathing argument for God. The old apologetics of previous generations assumed that the barrier to conversion was intellectual and the way to remove that barrier was to answer all cognitive doubts. But Xers live in an age of intellectual ambiguity, when cognitive answers carry considerably less weight. The question my generation asks is not "Can Christians prove what they believe?" but "Can Christians live what they believe?"[7]

There are some major themes in the Christian message which interface nicely with the Xer experience. If these can be presented in the right way, there is a good chance that many members of the X Generation will embrace the Christian message and make the church their family as their needs are met. Their needs become gateways which may open up their hearts to be receptive to the message of the gospel.

The Need For Community

Without a doubt the most popular sitcom with the Generation X crowd is "Friends." A curious observation about the program is that the characters are hardly ever doing anything of substance. We rarely see them at work or involved in some cause. The entire program consists of their hanging out at a coffee shop or in one of their apartments eating and dealing with some aspect of their interpersonal relationships with each other, former spouses or lovers.

Eating together has almost become a sacred activity with Generation X. It doesn't have to be at a fancy restaurant and it doesn't have to be a gourmet meal. It is the time spent together in bonding, sharing problems, and supporting one another that is pursued by this generation. I believe it is an attempt to create a spirit of family which most of them never had because their families were either dysfunctional or fragmented by divorce. Their friends have become their substitute family. With their special group of friends, they can say anything, do anything, and be anything — and they know they will still be accepted. Meal times are when the members of a family share the events of the day, work out problems and support one another. Generation X missed that and they are making up for that loss with their friends.

Randy,[8] a colleague of mine, was sharing with me his frustration about his little brother, Dave, who is a typical Xer. Both Randy and his mother find Dave's commitment to his friends hard to understand. When a holiday comes around, Randy and his mother try to arrange their schedules so that they can be together for some "family time." They find it hard to deal with the fact that Dave doesn't make the same effort, or that he places his friends' requests for time on the same par with the family. But if you would ask Dave about it, he would simply answer, "But my friends *are* my family."

I failed to mention that Randy and Dave's mother was divorced by their father when they were preteens. It was a rough time for them and Dave found solace and strength in his friends. His mother did the best she could as a single mother, but with a job and trying to keep up a house, she just didn't have the time or emotional energy to give to Dave as before. So Dave turned to his friends for support and they have been "family" to him as much, if not more, than his biological family.

> Americans have traditionally described "family" as all of the people who were related to each other by marriage, birth or adoption. No longer is this the prevailing definition, though. Several years ago we discovered that a majority of adults now define family to be any and all individuals whom they deeply care for or who deeply care about them. Not surprisingly, teenagers have now adopted the same perspective. Almost two out of three teens currently believe that this nouveau definition of family is the most accurate. They contend that it does not exclude individuals who are related by blood or marriage from being deemed family, but it does not automatically give them such preferred status. In other words, in our achievement-oriented society, there are no more free rides: if you want to be a part of the family, you have to earn it.[9]

Remember Stephanie, the girl whose mother said, "You are the worst $5,000 investment I ever made?" I had the privilege of visiting her and sharing with the youth sponsors and staff leadership in her church on Generation X. Saturday evening, after the seminars were over, she invited me to eat with some selected members of the Twentysomething group from the church. With great pride she went around and introduced me to every guest who was sitting around the living room eating her homemade enchiladas. After she finished making all the introductions, she motioned around the room where the guests were seated and said, "This is my family." The rejection and loneliness that she had struggled with for so long was being healed through being a part of this special community.

> In a culture like ours, where the individual is so dehumanized, the recovery of genuine humanity begins with the forming of real friendships. Friends genuinely care for one another. A friend

does not "use" the other person to achieve some goal — for example, befriending only those coworkers who might enhance one's chances of promotion. Friends trust each other. For Xers who have learned not to trust anyone, friendship is a decisive step in the direction of healing. . .[10]

	WHAT IS A FAMILY ACCORDING TO GENERATION X?
28%	People with whom you have close relationships or deep personal/emotional bonds
25%	Those individuals with whom you have a mutual personal commitment or love relationship
24%	Your good friends, those with whom you are compatible, those with whom there is mutual caring
23%	The people who are there for you to provide help or emotional support, as needed
21%	People who are related by marriage
19%	Individuals to whom you are closely related, by marriage or blood lines
11%	People who live together, regardless of their legal status
9%	All people with whom you have significant interaction
	Source: George Barna, *Baby Busters*

The church is pictured in many ways in the Scriptures; as a body, a family, a living temple and others. In order to effectively reach out to Generation X, it must be seen by them as a place of refuge, a retreat. It must be a haven from the pain, rejection and alienation they have experienced in the world. Life for the Xer can be extremely harsh. What is needed is an oasis. In their travels through life, the Xer will encounter many mirages in the form of pop-psychology, philosophy and false religions. What they need is to taste the genuine article, they need "living water."

Come, all you who are thirsty, come to the waters; and you who have no money, come, buy and eat! Come, buy wine and milk without money and without cost. Why spend money on what is not bread, and your labor on what does not satisfy? Listen, listen to me, and eat what is good, and your soul will delight in the richest of fare (Is 55:12).[11]

How will they find this living water? Through interaction

with genuine, caring Christians who live out the love of Christ in the context of an accepting, loving fellowship. Friendships and healing take place in the context of community. Restoration of community is a primary need for Generation X. What better place for that to happen than the body of Christ, the family of God? From the beginning, the church has been a caring and supportive community. In the book of Acts we read:

> They devoted themselves to the apostles' teaching and to the fellowship, to the breaking of bread and to prayer. Everyone was filled with awe, and many wonders and miraculous signs were done by the apostles. All the believers were together and had everything in common. Selling their possessions and goods, they gave to anyone as he had need. Every day they continued to meet together in the temple courts. They broke bread in their homes and ate together with glad and sincere hearts, praising God and enjoying the favor of all the people. And the Lord added to their number daily those who were being saved (Acts 2:42-47).

> All the believers were one in heart and mind. No one claimed that any of his possessions was his own, but they shared everything they had. With great power the apostles continued to testify to the resurrection of the Lord Jesus, and much grace was upon them all. There were no needy persons among them. For from time to time those who owned lands or houses sold them, brought the money from the sales and put it at the apostles' feet, and it was distributed to anyone as he had need (Acts 4:32-35).

Xers hold many things in common with one another already. Unfortunately, most of them are negative experiences — rejection, abuse, and fear. These needy souls are longing for the church to reach out in support and to offer healing grace in the form of a loving and supportive community. We already have a model of community given to us in the book of Acts. It is now simply a matter of the church getting past the brightly colored hair and weird haircuts and other insignificant differences to let the healing of Christ flow through outstretched arms offering a supportive hug or the willingness to walk hand in hand through the painful process of repentance, recovery and restoration.

Spirituality

As I have stated in previous chapters, Xers are very much interested in spiritual things. They feel a need for spiritual expression. Yet, they are not sure how to fulfill that longing. Hear the words of Douglas Coupland, author of *Generation X* and *Life After God*:

> Now — here is my secret: I tell it to you with an openness of heart that I doubt I shall ever achieve again, so I pray that you are in a quiet room as you hear these words. My secret is that I need God — that I am sick and can no longer make it alone. I need God to help me give, because I no longer seem to be capable of giving; to help me be kind, as I no longer seem capable of kindness; to help me love, as I seem beyond being able to love.[12]

While Xers have spiritual needs and are interested in spiritual issues, they are not necessarily confining their spiritual search to Christianity. For Xers, New Age, Eastern mysticism, Native American religious practices, Buddhism and many other religious beliefs are considered legitimate sources to investigate in their search for spiritual insight and meaning.

The church needs to rise to the challenge of finding effective ways to communicate the story of Christ so that it will be considered by those who are searching for answers to their spiritual questions. Because society reflects a postmodern culture, which is post-Christian in nature, one must not assume that any member of Generation X has an adequate understanding of the Judeo-Christian God and the biblical message of salvation. So where does one start?

Once again, I believe that we have the perfect model in the book of Acts. In the seventeenth chapter, the apostle Paul has arrived in the city of Athens which was one of the intellectual and cultural centers of his day. He has been invited to explain his religious beliefs to the council of the Areopagus, a group of philosophical intellectuals. On his way, he had noticed a statue which had been erected "to an unknown god." Paul centered his message on the worship of the True God, whom the Athenians were already worshipping, albeit through ignorance and superstition. He drew upon their innate religious hunger, which had been demonstrated by the presence of this statue, and used it as a bridge to share the story of Christ.

Perhaps the most effective thing that the Christian can do to share Christ with a member of Generation X, is to acknowledge and appreciate their interest in spiritual matters. Recognize the good that is already there. The next step would be to live out the claims of the Christian life in their midst and to share in an understandable way who God is and how one comes to know him.

The Christian must help the Xer to see and understand what authentic Christianity is as presented in the New Testament. They need to acquire a clear picture of the model church without all of the cultural baggage that has been tacked on to it down through the ages. Sometimes our traditions and man-made rituals obscure the true and essential elements of the faith. For example, Xers are turned off by the slick, highly polished, success-oriented, God wants you to be rich and successful pseudo-religious presentation of many TV evangelists, and rightly so.

But TV evangelists are not the only offenders. Fundamentalists, in their zeal to honor Scripture, often come across as harsh, condemning and lacking grace and compassion. The substitution of psycho-babble instead of Scripture which fills many liberal pulpits does nothing to fill the spiritual longing within the soul of Generation X.

Because the decaying values of modernity has left man without any significance or meaning, people have a great need to be a part of something larger than themselves. The body of Christ is alive and as each member uses his or her gifts to enhance the overall outreach and ministry of the church, they become an integral part of a dynamic community which has the power to transform the culture. In the body of Christ one's focus changes from "me-centered" to "we-centered." One's identification with the body of Christ gives meaning and significance in a way not possible by oneself.

There have been some very encouraging and very significant spiritual movements rise up from among Generation X which are worth noting. Mars Hill Productions has made a new film series documenting these exciting events within Generation X.[13] In 1984 President Reagan enacted the Equal Access Act. This gave students the right to use a classroom after school for prayer and Bible study if it was student led. No teachers were allowed to participate, because it was feared that it would be seen as promoting a particular religion and the government wanted to maintain the separation of church and state. One might think that without teachers or other adults to promote and lead the Bible studies, that they would not even get off the ground. Au contraire! Over 10,000 of them exist on school campuses all across the nation.

Closely related to the student led prayer and Bible study clubs is a movement called "See You at the Pole." It began in the spring of 1990 in a small Texas town and has now grown to include thousands of students all across the nation. On a chosen day at the beginning of a new school year, Christian students all over America will meet around their school's flagpole before school to join hands and to pray for boldness in witnessing and for God's blessing upon their school and their lives. In the beginning, some were even arrested and jailed for their efforts. Schools tried to halt the event by citing separation of church and state. But the students remained committed to their desire to take a public stand for their faith and eventually they were granted permission to do so because it comes under the protection of the laws guaranteeing free speech.

Another significant spiritual movement started by Christian members of Generation X is the "True Love Waits" campaign. It started in the spring of 1993 with just 53 students who took a

173

public pledge to remain sexually pure until marriage. In just two years this message of holiness and purity swept through the churches and youth groups of the land. Over one hundred thousand young people of Generation X attended rallies and signed commitment cards to uphold sexual purity in their lives. This is an incredible turn around from the sexual promiscuity of their parents' generation — the free love era of the '60s.

Every summer a large number of students go off to serve in short-term mission projects. Many of them have never met before, but their desire to do something that makes a difference brings them together. They build houses in Mexico, teach underprivileged children in the inner cities of Chicago, Atlanta, and New York. The gospel is taken to the poor in Haiti, India and Thailand. All over the globe young members of Generation X are volunteering in record numbers. On May 20, 1995, in South Korea, over 60,000 college students pledged to dedicate an entire year of their life to spreading the gospel before establishing their own careers and starting a family.

Sexuality

Generation X has a passion for the practical, for that which works. They are not interested in theological controversies, denominational differences, or legalistic hair splitting over nonessential issues. They have a survival mindset which is seeking a faith that will "work" in the real world. They need something that will make a practical difference in their everyday lives. Xers are very results oriented and a faith that doesn't tangibly improve their lives and make a difference in some way is going to be quickly discarded.

One very important area where the church can be very helpful is in the area of sexuality. "A 1981 Guttmacher Institute study showed that by age twenty, 81 percent of unmarried males and 60 percent of unmarried females have engaged in sexual intercourse."[14] Many of these became sexually active as early as age eleven. One reason for Xers' early sexual involve-

174

ment is because society as a whole has become more tolerant of sexual expression outside of marriage. With the abandonment of belief in absolutes in our cultures, teens are not given any practical reasons for *not* giving in to their sexual desires other than cautions concerning sexually transmitted diseases and unwanted pregnancy.

But as I have talked with numerous teens who are sexually active, my distinct impression is that most of them are looking for something much deeper than just a quick sexual encounter. Most are looking for affection — for the love that was absent in their familial relationships. This is especially true of young teenage girls who have absent or neglectful fathers.[15] With all of the broken homes and working parents, could it be that most Xers simply never received enough affection through traditional means and that they are merely seeking to fill a void in their life through their sexual encounters?

God's standards for sexuality have people's best interests at the heart of them. Xers must be shown that God is not some cosmic killjoy by insisting that people live holy lives and only express their sexuality within the bonds of marriage, but is acting as a caring and compassionate father by trying to spare them from greater pain caused by illicit sexual involvement. One place this is clearly seen is in the effects of cohabitation.

According to government statistics for 1986, there were more than 2.2 million couples who cohabitated, or lived together outside the bonds of marriage. That is a significant increase from the half million who lived together in 1970. Nationwide, 44% of all couples married between 1980 and 1984 cohabited before marriage, compared to only 11% in the years between 1965-1974.[16]

Many Xers see cohabitation as a way of "trying out a marriage" before actually being married to make sure that it will work. Because of the trauma they were forced to endure because of their parents' divorce, they seek ways to insure that they will not do the same to their kids. They believe that living together before marriage will help insure a stronger and more successful relationship. But as cohabitation becomes more popular and accepted, researchers are finding that the practice does not fulfill expectations.

Of the couples who lived together between 1975 and 1984, about 70% eventually married. But contrary to their hopes and expectations, cohabitation did not make for stronger marriages. In a national study by researchers from the University of Wisconsin it was found that the divorce rate over a 10 year period ran one-third *higher* among couples who had lived together before marriage than among couples who had not.[17]

Even among those couples who stayed together, it was found that those who did not cohabitate before marriage find greater happiness than those who have. A study by researchers from both Auburn and the University of Florida found that both spouses of those couples who had lived together before marriage rated their satisfaction level with their relationship *lower* than those who had not cohabitated.

Many other significant insights have been gained by studying the effects of cohabitation. Cohabitating women are almost five times as likely to suffer severe violence from their partners as married women. Cohabitation does not foster deep and lasting commitments like marriage does. A cohabitating women is much more likely than a married woman to end up providing the economic support for an unemployed man.[18]

In every significant area it is seen that cohabitation does not help guarantee the success of a relationship, but actually works against it. For the pragmatic minded members of Generation X, this is powerful information. It can be used to illustrate the wisdom and practicality of God's standards and the rewards for following them.

Mystery

Xers live in a postmodern culture and operate from a postmodern mindset. They are fascinated by mystery — things that cannot be explained by rational argument or scientific observation. As Christians, we need not apologize for our belief in the supernatural, unfathomable nature of God. Instead, we can emphasize the mystery, awe and transcendence of God without feeling that we must have a degree in apologetics and philosophy in order to justify and carry on the discussion. Because Xers are comfortable with mystery, Christians can share the mystery of the incarnation and use it as a means of explaining the great love that God has for all people.

The New Testament uses the word "mystery" about twenty-five times, once in the Gospels (Mark 4:11; compare Matt. 13:11; Luke 8:10), twenty-one times in Paul's writings, and a few times in Revelation. The way that mystery is understood in the New Testament is as a "sacred secret" where matters previously kept secret in God's eternal purposes have now been or are being revealed (Eph. 3:3-5; 1 Cor. 2:7-8). The central focus of mystery in the New Testament centers around the historical activity of the person of Christ (Col. 2:2; Eph. 1:9) and the indwelling Christ is the hope of glory for the individual Christian (Col. 1:26-27). The mystery is received spiritually (Eph. 3:4-5) and manifested in the proclamation of the gospel (Eph. 6:19). Part of the mystery involves the disclosure that Gentiles share in the blessings of the gospel (Eph. 2:11-13).[19]

Paul compares the love that Christ has for the church with the love that is shared between a husband and wife in a marriage relationship. He refers to it as a "profound mystery" (Eph 5:32). Why God should love us so is a mystery, but it is a truth nonetheless. Because Generation X has been unwanted, abused and rejected, they should be very open to the unconditional love of God. But they must encounter it through caring, healing relationships. They are not going to be reached if they only hear it preached — it must be lived out by people who wear the name of Christian.

Relationships Versus Race and Possessions

Xers place a high value upon their friendships. This emphasis

177

upon the importance of relationships has ramifications that reach out into other significant areas. First of all, Xers are the most ethnically diverse and racially tolerant generation in American history. They accept, respect and socialize with one another much more than any earlier generations of differing backgrounds. One way this is clearly demonstrated is by the 300% increase in black-white married couples over the last twenty years.[20] The color of one's skin is not as much of an issue for Generation X as it was for previous generations. Xers are just more accepting — they care more about what is on the inside than a person's outward appearance.

That unconditional acceptance is at the heart of the gospel. One of the first songs that I learned as a young child sitting in Sunday School was "Jesus Loves the Little Children." "Jesus loves the little children, *all* the children of the world, red, brown, yellow, black and white, they are precious in his sight . . . ." Paul writes in Galatians 3:28, "There is neither Jew nor Greek, slave nor free, male nor female, for you are all one in Christ Jesus." It is time we live out what we sing and preach.

Unfortunately, if the church is going to try and use this as a bridge for reaching Generation X, most local congregations will have to dedicate some time for a period of reflection and repentance because the hour between 11:00 a.m. and 12:00 p.m. on Sunday morning is still the most segregated spot in the nation. Most members of our youth groups will come into contact with more people of different races and cultures at school than they will at church. This is to our shame. The great commission is to proclaim that forgiveness of sins is available for *all* people, of *all* races and cultures. The Promise Keepers movement has recognized this offense and one of the seven promises of a Promise Keeper is to be committed to reaching beyond any racial barriers to demonstrate the power of biblical unity.[21] The church must return to an all-inclusive acceptance of people regardless of their race or cultural background if it is going to have any appeal to Generation X.

Another area in which Generation X places a priority upon

people is in the business world. It has been accepted for years, especially by Boomers, that it is a "dog eat dog" world out there. That means that you must do anything and everything to get ahead in business, even if it means going behind a coworker's back or cheating a business partner out of a deal.

Most Xers refuse to accept this as standard operating procedure. They are determined to "eat less dog" so to speak. By that, I mean that they refuse to place career advancement or pay raises ahead of their relationships with their coworkers. It just is not worth it to live in that kind of world. They have seen what that mindset did to their parents' lives — and they want none of it.

Over and over the prophets decry the practice of exploiting people for personal profit. Amos 2:6 says "This is what the LORD says: "For three sins of Israel, even for four, I will not turn back my wrath. They sell the righteous for silver, and the needy for a pair of sandals." God's people need to practice and lift high his standard of placing people and their needs over things. Generation X is already committed to following this ideal — it should be an easy transition to move them from the ideal to the one who embodies the ideal — Jehovah God.

A typical Xer's attitude about work is also going to reflect his passion for relationships over material possessions. This is in great contrast to the attitude of the previous generation. A typical Boomer would sell his soul to the company to work his way up the corporate ladder. Sixteen hour days, eighty hour weeks, and working lunches were all worth the price for the Boomer because his goal was to gain wealth — material possessions. He wanted the BMW, Armani suits, the condo with the hot-tub, and Caribbean vacations and was willing to pay whatever the price in order to achieve this goal. Most Boomers believed the lie (or at least lived as though they did) that money and possessions will bring happiness. Their motto was, "He who dies with the most toys wins."

This is what separates Boomers from Xers. Generation X was neglected by their parents in pursuit of the American Dream —

they were the casualties of this materialistic lust. Their parents were too busy pursuing their careers to spend time playing with their children or attending their functions so Xers grew up learning to lean on and cherish each other. Friends became the family they never had. Therefore, their desire is to spend their time doing things with each other, just hanging out and enjoying one another's company. From this fellowship they draw strength and support.

For the Xer, a job is simply a necessary evil. They only want to do what is absolutely necessary to sustain a simple lifestyle that allows them to spend the most time hanging out with their friends and pursuing what they believe is most important in life. They have no desire to work longer hours or any overtime. "Boomers live to work, while Busters work to live."[22] Boomers, to a large degree, derive their identity and self-esteem from what they accomplish on the job. Busters or Xers only see the job as a means to an end.

The Christian's view of a career is more similar to that of the Xer than that of the Boomer. The New Testament decries the pursuit of wealth over the neglect of one's soul.

> "No servant can serve two masters. Either he will hate the one and love the other, or he will be devoted to the one and despise the other. You cannot serve both God and Money." The Pharisees, who loved money, heard all this and were sneering at Jesus. He said to them, "You are the ones who justify yourselves in the eyes of men, but God knows your hearts. What is highly valued among men is detestable in God's sight" (Luke 16:13-15).

God's people should see their primary vocation as serving Jesus. This makes a profound difference in how they approach their jobs.

> For Christians, life's primary vocation is ministry. Christians view their workplace as a ministry post. Their pulpits are their desks, their cars, their classrooms, their kitchens. Seeing oneself as a mine worker, homemaker, school teacher, or professional person who happens to be a Christian is fundamentally different

from seeing oneself primarily as a Christian who happens to be a secretary, salesperson, or accountant. A proper theology of work operating in the lives of believers would see many people positively influenced toward Christ in every setting where Christians are found working.[23]

Family

Because so many members of Generation X are children of divorced and dysfunctional families, they are fiercely committed to restoring a healthy family model for their own children. I can't tell you how many times I have heard a member of Generation X say, "I am going to make my marriage work, no matter what. I will never put my kids through what I went through when my parents divorced."

Not only have Xers had their families disintegrate in record numbers through divorce, but many have grown up in a violent environment. Thirty percent of married couples experience domestic violence, with two million of these couples using a lethal weapon on each other. Every year three to four million wives are beaten by their husbands, and at least a thousand die.[24]

I was talking to David,[25] a young father of six children, at a church social after a Sunday night revival meeting. The conversation turned to my research on Generation X. He was curious because he was a part of the first wave of Generation X. He shared with me his family background. In many ways he fits the typical profile for an Xer.

His parents divorced when he was eleven. He said that he had never seen such hate between two people but what was exhibited between his father and mother during the divorce. They almost burned up (literally) everything that was of value in the home. If his mother came across anything that his father wanted or liked, she actually started a fire in the yard and threw whatever was of value into the fire that her ex-husband wanted. His father did the same. There wasn't much left after the battle encounters between his mother and father. About the only thing that he had of value was a set of matchbox cars and trucks. Those all got burned up in the fire. He has nothing of his childhood to share with his own children.

The good news in all of this is that you would never guess that he has such a painful past by watching him relate to his own family. He and his wife have chosen to have a large family of their own, and they dearly love their children. Every one of them is precious. David volunteers to help with Junior Church, Sunday School, and youth group. He has not allowed his own painful past to keep him from having a happy, healthy family of his own.

This has not come about by accident. It is a matter of choice and design. David has vowed that his kids would not suffer like he did. In the power of Christ and the supportive nurture of the church, David found a substitute family that was able to bring about healing in his own life and supply a model and a context for healthy family relationships. I believe that David represents the desire of most Xers when it comes to family. They are committed to making it work.

> Thirteeners will establish marriages that are far more stable and enduring than those of their oft-divorced parents. And. . . they will become extremely protective parents, seeking to shield their children from the harsh realities they experienced growing up.[26]

Howe and Strauss, in their classic work, *13th Gen: Abort, Retry, Ignore, Fail*, predict that Generation X will restrengthen the American family. They will accomplish this by protecting their own marriages from the stress of their work lives by not allowing work to consume more of their time than is absolutely essential to get the job done.

> First as parents and later as community leaders, 13ers will practice and advocate a heavily protective, even smothering style of nurture. They will revive the innocence of childhood by deliberately shielding their own kids from the harsher realities of life, and by prohibiting those kids from taking the same liberties they themselves once took at the same age.[27]

182

While the goal of desiring healthier, more stable families is noble, those of us who have raised our families are aware of the fact that just *wanting* them to be healthy is not sufficient in and of itself to make it happen. There must be healthy communication, shared ideals, and a commitment to make it so.

Generation X lacked the proper models to teach them how to build a healthy family because so many of their families were dysfunctional in one way or another. If they are to be successful in their desire to build healthy families, they will need some good examples to follow and instructional insights on how to go about constructing a healthy family.

This is where the church comes in. By offering classes on parenting and marriage enrichment, the church will fill a very practical need in the life of the Xer. (Remember, Xers are very big on what is practical, on what works.) The families of church leaders and members will serve as examples for those who are seeking a model of a healthy family. The church family becomes a sort of "para-family" for the Xer. It comes alongside and fills in where his own nuclear family is deficient.

One of the healthiest moves that has been made in the church in the past years is the move towards family ministry and family-based youth ministry. After years of working with youth in isolation, churches have finally come to the realization that the family is the primary molder of values and character. Churches are now incorporating the entire family in worship events and social activities. Special classes on parenting and family enrichment are being offered. For those who would like to know more about how to incorporate family concerns into the overall ministry of the church I would recommend the book of my good friend, Steve Thomas, *Your Church Can Be. . . Family Friendly: How You Can Launch a Successful Family Ministry in Your Congregation* and *Family-Based Youth Ministry* by Mark DeVries.[28]

Psalm 68:5-6 says: "A father to the fatherless, defender of widows is God in his holy dwelling. God sets the lonely in families, he leads forth the prisoners with singing; but the rebellious live in a sun-scorched land." Notice that the text says that God sets the lonely in families. It could have said that God sets the lonely in clubs, or on teams, or in a job, or in the city. But God's solution for healing lonely people, is not in having them join a club, an athletic team or attend some social function — it is getting connected to a family. Healing takes place in families and the church is to be the surrogate family for those who have lost or never had the kind of supportive relationship and community needed to foster growth and fulfillment.

Identity

Part of the struggle for Generation X is the struggle for an identity. They were unwanted and neglected as children. They are shunned and discounted by society today as a bunch of "slackers" and "apathetic rejects." The result is that they have a troubling fear that they really are worthless as human beings.

> As a class, our self-esteem if low. The prevalence of body art (tattoos) on both young men and young women suggests a lack of self-respect and self-esteem. To Xers the body is no longer a temple. It is just another bare wall upon which to scrawl our graffiti.[29]

Historically, people have tried all kinds of things in search of their identity. They have tried meditation, joined fitness clubs, called psychic hot-lines, est, tarot cards and astrology. They have made pilgrimages to holy places and participated in group marathon sessions at the Esalen Institute at Big Sur. None of these have fully satisfied. That is because one's identity or the self is not waiting to be discovered — it is waiting to be created. The secret to a healthy self-esteem and identity is understanding the principle that you are what you commit yourself to. The self is waiting to be created.

In 2 Kings 17:15 the Bible says, ". . . They followed worthless idols and themselves became worthless." God punished the ten northern tribes of Israel by sending them into Assyrian captivity. This is because they had made themselves worthless by their abandonment of God's covenant and their commitment to idolatry. You are what you commit yourself to.

The positive side of this is that there is great hope for Generation X if they commit themselves to Christ and identify themselves with His kingdom. Paul writes in 2 Corinthians 3:18, "And we, who with unveiled faces all reflect the Lord's glory, are being transformed into his likeness with ever-increasing glory, which comes from the Lord, who is the Spirit." In Ephesians 4:22-24 he writes, "You were taught, with regard to your former way of life, to put off your old self, which is being corrupted by its deceitful desires; to be made new in the attitude of your minds; and to put on the new self, created to be like God in true righteousness and holiness." Colossians 3:9-10 says, "Do not lie to each other, since you have taken off your old self with its practices and have put on the new self, which is being renewed in knowledge in the image of its Creator." All of these verses are filled with the hope and promise that we can become something greater and finer than what we are naturally. On our own, we are sinners, lost and without hope in the world. But we do not have to remain in this state; we can become like Christ when we choose to identify with him.

Involvement In Causes

Boomers liked to get involved in causes. They protested the Vietnam War and marched for civil rights. They believed that they could change the world. They organized sit-ins and sang protest songs. These young Boomers enjoyed the limelight and wanted the world to take notice of them and their causes.

It is these same Boomers who have grown up to be "the establishment" and the very same ones who look down on Xers and consider them to be a generation of apathetic slackers with no ideals, beliefs or causes. This is a totally untrue and invalid judgment against Generation X.

Generation X wants to make a difference in the world also, but their methodology is different. Boomers were involved in

185

large concerns such as world peace, world hunger, poverty and the environment. Xers are just as concerned, but their concerns are on more of a local level. Not only do they want to make a difference, but they want to be able *to see* the difference they are making. In order to accomplish this, they involve themselves in local causes which are not likely to make the 6 o'clock news or the cover of *Time* or *Newsweek* as are national or international causes. But that is fine with the typical Xer. He doesn't care for rhetoric anyway — that is his criticism of the Boomer establishment — too much talk and not enough action. But just because they don't make the front page, do not assume that Xers are not concerned or uninvolved.

> Nearly half volunteer their time to help needy people in their area. Critically important, though is the realization that much of the volunteerism happens apart from organization-driven efforts; that is, Busters will lend a hand to the needy on their own, or in conjunction with friends and family who share the desire to make a difference.[30]

The church needs to recognize and acknowledge the spirit of volunteerism that is present in Generation X and provide avenues for individuals to plug into the life and mission of the church in a meaningful way. Realize that Xers (at least at first) are not very likely to be motivated to contribute to a missions organization which is promoting some need in a distant place. Xers want to be able to see the results of their contributions. That goes for monetary contributions as well as their personal involvement of labor and sweat. An Xer is much more likely to help out at a local soup kitchen to feed the homeless than he is to contribute money to a World Vision project to help the needy in the Sudan. This does not mean that one should ignore worldwide mission needs, but it is only a recognition of the fact that entry level involvement for Xers is going to start locally at first. As they grow in their faith, they will be willing to reach out to those across the seas in foreign lands.

The biblical concept of each member of the church being like the part of a body will appeal to the typical Xer. He is looking for individual participation and involvement. Paul's teaching about the body underscores the fact that every Christian's contribution is needed and important if the church is to fulfill her mission. Every Christian has a gift, and no one's gift is to be despised and looked down upon by the other members of the body of Christ.[31]

Conclusion

As one can see, there are a number of gateways to the soul of Generation X. It is now up to the church to utilize those natural bridges which exist and open up the door to the heart of a searching generation. If the church is to be successful in this endeavor, it must make some changes in its programming and structure which reflect an understanding of the world and needs of Generation X. The next chapter will deal with the specific program needs and changes that are necessary to be effective in reaching the next generation.

Life Application and Implication For Ministry

1. Tape a presentation of the popular sitcom "Friends" (edit out all of the commercials) and show it at a youth group meeting or retreat. Have the teens identify all of the issues that they can relate to in their own lives. Brainstorm together and try to come up with as many ideas as you can for ways in which the church might address and help teens deal with those specific issues.

2. If eating together is such a priority for members of Generation X, then make sure that your youth group meetings and social functions have a time for refreshments and fellowship. Be sure to allow for adequate time so that the sharing time is not rushed. You may even want to revive the old social idea of a progressive dinner as one of your yearly events.

3. Ask the members of your youth group to write down their definition of "family." Make a master list of all of the definitions

and compare the responses for similarities and differences. Did they just include people who were biologically related to them, or did they include stepfamily relationships? Friends?

4. In what ways does your church as a family? How do members communicate love and concern for one another? What evens do they participate in as a family?

5. Take a poll of the members of your youth group. Ask them to rate their openness (1 is low and 10 is high) to receiving wisdom or insight about life and spiritual issues from the following sources:

___ Mormonism ___ Buddhism ___ New Age
___ Psychology ___ Philosophy ___ Mysticism
___ Astrology ___ Tarot cards ___ Catholicism
___ Native American Religion ___ Occult
___ Psychic hot lines

6. Encourage your youth group members to start a Bible Club at their school or to support the one that is there. Challenge them to take a leadership position.

7. Find out when the local "See You At the Pole" rally is scheduled and encourage the members of your youth group to support it and participate in the prayer time.

8. What short-term mission projects are available for the members of your youth group and church to participate in? If you have never organized a short-term missions trip, then I would recommend that you contact Steve Sigler at Christ In Youth (Box B, Joplin, MO 64802) and request information on all of the mission trips that they offer. Christ In Youth offers both inner city projects and overseas short-term missions projects at a very reasonable price.

9. What can your church do to promote better race relationships in your community? If there is a black congregation nearby, consider being involved in a Sunday pulpit exchange to facilitate and promote growth and understanding between the two congregations.

10. What causes are the members of your youth group most likely to participate in?

___ Feed the homeless   ___ Hospital volunteer work
___ Tutoring   ___ Special Olympics
___ Environmental clean-up   ___ Unicef
___ Big Brother/Big Sister   ___ Walk for Crop

Notes

1. Douglas Coupland, *Life After God*, 273-274.

2. Andres Tapia, "Reaching The First Post-Christian Generation," *Christianity Today*, 12 September 1994, 20.

3. Jarrett Kerbel, "Generation's Faith," *Sojourners*, November 1994, 15.

4. Piper Lowell, "Generation's Faith," *Sojourners*, November 1994, 20.

5. Listen to the lyrics or read the words to Alanis Morissette's song "Ironic" on her *Jagged Little Pill* CD or tape, 1995 MCA Music.

6. Issues such as the environment and the national debt are particularly hot issues with Generation X. They believe that previous generations have recklessly depleted our natural resources, polluted our rivers and beaches, and have built up the national debt to a point that it is almost impossible to ever pay it. On top of all that is the staggering liability of Social Security with more and more people retiring and withdrawing money from the system with fewer and fewer people able to put in enough to keep up with the rate of withdrawal.

7. Kevin Graham Ford, *Jesus For a New Generation*, 174.

8. Not his real name, but used with permission.

9. George Barna, *Generation Next*, 49.

10. William Mahedy & Janet Bernardi, *A Generation Alone*, 80.

11. See also: Psalm 107:4-9 and John 4:10-15.

12. Douglas Coupland, *Life After God*, 359.

13. For more information about renting this excellent series contact: Mars Hill Productions, 12705 South Kirkwood STE. 218, Stafford, Texas 77477 or phone them at 713-240-6474.

14. Josh McDowell, *How To Help Your Child Say "No" To Sexual Pressure* (Waco, TX: Word Books, 1987), 10.

15. See ibid., 33-34 for a personal testimony about a young girl who realized that her sexual activity was related to her search for her daddy's love.

16. Bryce Christensen, "Cohabitation Fails Expectations," *The Joplin Globe*, 5 November 1989, p. 6A.

17. Ibid.

18. Ibid.

19. Tommy Brisco, "Mystery Religions," Holman Bible Dictionary, Quick Verse (Hiawatha, IA: Parsons Technology).

20. Geoffrey T. Holt, *Welcome to the Jungle*, 207.

21. Al Janssen and Larry K. Weeden, eds. *Seven Promises of a Promise Keeper* (Colorado Springs, CO: Focus on the Family Publishing, 1994), 153.

22. George Barna, *Baby Busters*, 101.

23. T.R. McNeal, "Work, Theology of," Holman Bible Dictionary, Quick Verse (Hiawatha, IA: Parsons Technology).

24. Franci Smith and Susan Coleman, "Battered Women," The New Grolier Electronic Encyclopedia, The Software Toolworks, Inc, 1993, paragraph 1.

25. Not his real name, but used with permission.

26. Bill Marvel and Melissa Morrison, "The Pacifier People," *The Dallas Morning News*, F4, quoted in Gary L. McIntosh, *Three Generations: Riding the Waves of Change in Your Church* (Grand Rapids: Fleming H. Revell, 1995), 145.

27. Neil Howe and Bill Strauss, *13th Gen*, 221.

28. Steve Thomas, *Your Church Can Be . . . Family Friendly: How You Can Launch a Successful Family Ministry in Your Congregation*, Joplin, MO: College Press, 1996, and Mark DeVries, *Family-Based Youth Ministry*, Downers Grove, IL: InterVarsity Press, 1994.

29. Ford, *Jesus for a New Generation*, 25.

30. Barna, *Baby Busters*, 81-82.

31. See: I Corinthians 12:12-31; Romans 12:3-8; Ephesians 4:11-13.

Programming to Meet the Needs
of Generation X

Thirteeners are very open to the Christian story right now — if it is presented in an effective and appropriate way. They may be closed to old, outmoded evangelistic methods, but not to the story itself. — Kevin Graham Ford in *Jesus For a New Generation: Putting the Gospel in the Language of Xers*[1]

What we label the drug problem, the teen pregnancy problem, and the host of other problems of youth are merely the symptoms of a much larger, deep-rooted, and serious dilemma. Today's youth are at risk simply because they have no satisfactory reason to live. — Fran Sciacca in *Generation At Risk: What Legacy Are the Baby-Boomers Leaving Their Kids?*[2]

The Word of God anticipates the dilemma of our age and for our church in the profound question of Psalm 11:3; "When the foundations are being destroyed, what can the righteous do?" Our whole modern era has been engaged in destroying foundations and in trying to erect some new foundation on the rubble. — Gene Edward Veith, Jr. in *Postmodern Times: A Christian Guide to Contemporary Thought and Culture*[3]

Successful youth ministry in this era certainly doesn't require bigger and better programs; rather, kids are looking for simplicity and effectiveness. Instead of building a Rolls-Royce with all the amenities, we need to build a simple Jeep — rugged, durable, and flexible. Your most effective planning tool may be your eraser. — Tim Smith in *Youthworker*[4]

Stand in awe of the Creator? Again, we find that the practical nature of millions of teenagers renders them more likely to stand in awe of the natural talents of Michael Jordan, the physical strength and grace of Shaquille O'Neal, the dexterity of Eddie Van Halen, and the physical beauty of Cindy Crawford or Claudia Schiffer than to bow down to the immeasurable capacity of God. — George Barna in *Generation Next: What Every Parent and Youthworker Needs to Know About the Attitudes and Beliefs of Today's Youth*[5]

A lot of people are turned off by Generation X. They have a hard time understanding their attraction to body piercing, tattoos, weird haircuts and their "grunge" style of dress. Because they can't understand them, they tend to either avoid them or criticize them. This has only contributed to the widening of the gap between the generations. A "me versus them" mentality threatens to further polarize Xers from previous generations.

For the generation that has been characterized by rejection and abandonment, what they don't need is further criticism. They need people who will sincerely care about the problems in their lives, and who are willing to invest their time in developing relationships that will allow healing to take place.

The church of the 21st century must rise to meet this challenge. As was pointed out in the previous chapter, there are a number of approaches for Christians to utilize that will serve as effective means of opening up dialogue with the members of Generation X. Xers feel alienated from their families and society as a whole. The Christian experience is about reconciliation.[6] Xers also lack a defined identity. A brand new identity is available to them if they will seize the opportunity and embrace Christ. They are battered and broken. In the church they will discover a healing community who will point them to Christ who understands what it means to be "despised and rejected . . . a man of sorrows, and familiar with suffering."[7] Generation X feels unwanted and unneeded. The church offers them a place of belonging, a place of involvement, a place where they can use their gifts and experiences in service of a purpose that is far greater than themselves. But this won't happen automatically. The typical church is going to have to make some adjustments in attitude and approach if it is going to be effective in reaching out to Generation X. ". . . we can't use yesterday's tools in today's world and expect to build a church for tomorrow."[8]

Creating a User-Friendly Environment

When most Xers walk into a typical church, they encounter

rituals and traditions that are totally foreign to them and make no sense whatsoever to their frame of reference. The stained glass windows, pipe organ music, and robed choirs don't have any connection with their world. It doesn't seem real. They don't readily see any application of what is going on in the sanctuary to what takes place in their everyday lives. The traditions and rituals of the service are mystifying to them, especially if they have no church background.

In light of this, it is a good idea to explain everything you do so that the unchurched guests will have some idea of what is going on and be able to respond appropriately. Those in charge of leading the worship should eliminate "churchy" sounding words from their vocabulary (like foyer, vestibule, and sanctuary) when making announcements and giving directions and replace them with common terms such as lobby, platform and auditorium. The one bringing the message should also avoid using theological jargon such as "sanctified," "redeemed," "born again" and "justified" and use terms that the man on the street would know and be comfortable with.

Bill went to a church service as a favor to a friend. His parents had never gone to church and he really had no idea about what to expect. When communion was passed, he watched the others partake so he took some when it came to him. When asked how he liked the church service after it was over he replied, "It was okay I guess, but can you explain to me why such friendly people are so stingy with the refreshments?" (Of course, he was referring to the communion.)

Another way to make the worship service more user friendly to the Xer is to "dress down." Xers are very casual and informal and feel out of place in the midst of a lot of "suits." The congregation will have to learn to be comfortable with seeing jeans, shorts and baseball caps in the sanctuary without feeling offended. The best way to communicate acceptance of a more casual dress is for those in leadership to set the example by modeling a more informal attire. You should also play down official titles and use first names when addressing people.

Xers like creativity and excitement. They do not want to *observe* a worship service as much as they want to *participate* in it. A seeker-service style of worship is probably best suited to generate an interest in Generation X and in getting them to have some sense of ownership in what is happening in the church. Seeker services are generally characterized by the use of contemporary music, both Christian and appropriate secular, praise bands, drama, comedy, film clips and multi-media presentations. The more places that can be generated for a person to serve, the more appealing it will be to the Xer. Seek out their input and suggestions and involve them in as many ways as you can in the service.

Not only does the worship service need to be of high quality, but it needs to flow smoothly, quickly and not drag on. Xers are the MTV generation. They have grown up with short, action-filled sound bites to keep their attention. They were practically born with a TV remote in their hands. If a show doesn't keep their interest, they will switch channels without giving it a second thought. While they can't exactly do this to a worship service that doesn't meet their standards, they do feel free to "switch channels" and attend church elsewhere the next Sunday.

While Xers desire to participate in a service, they do not want to be conspicuous in doing so. Do not call attention to them as guests — they want to participate anonymously, at least at first. But, they do not want to go completely unnoticed either. "Welcome them as a group, invite them to sit back and enjoy the service, and direct them to a welcome center for further information and refreshments."[9]

Be sure and make a good first impression. Xers are unsure about churches in the first place. "They will make a decision about your church within thirty seconds of entering the front door, so make that first thirty seconds good."[10] You should have a friendly person ready to greet them and direct them to the appropriate class or pew the moment they enter the building. Provide refreshments for them in the classrooms. This helps to set up a more informal atmosphere and promotes interaction between class members and guests.

Another very important way that your church can be user-friendly to the Xer is by providing excellent child-care facilities. It may be that about seventy-five percent of the Xers who attend your services are single and have no need of a nursery, but the twenty-five percent who are married or have children want superior facilities for their children. They will not leave them in a small, dingy, overcrowded and understaffed nursery. The facility should be an adequate size for the estimated number of children who need to be taken care of, and the furniture and play equipment should be high quality.

> Effective churches will attempt to convey the message of the Gospel in a manner that is understandable to contemporary culture. The key to conveying the truth and the claims of Christ is building effective bridges of communication and understanding between believers and nonbelievers.[11]

Every generation must have the gospel translated into its unique cultural context. To translate the gospel means to make an application of the eternal principles found in the text to the lives of the listeners in contemporary culture. However, with reference to the gospel message, *translation* is not the same as *transformation*. Transformation means to take the text and force it to say something that it was never intended to say. It is the imposing of one's preconceived ideas and agenda upon the text. While translation of the gospel message is a necessity, transformation of it must be avoided at all costs.

> The Gospel has always been contextualized. In our modern world, method and style must be brought kicking and screaming into the twenty-first century or else we will lose our full potential for reaching the postmodern Generation X and beyond for Christ. While the message is timeless, the method is not, and we've confused traditionalism with orthodoxy far too long.[12]

The members of Generation X are looking for messages that tell them how to be successful in life, how to handle all of the stresses and problems that they have encountered. Therefore, the preaching should be of a very practical nature. They care very little about theological issues and doctrinal differences. They are looking for a faith that will make a practical difference in their everyday lives and in their communities. They are very results-oriented, and a faith that doesn't tangibly improve their lives and immediate surroundings is going to be quickly discarded.

Xers are very comfortable with change. They don't like to conform to the traditional ways of doing things. They seek variety and diversity. A user-friendly church will try to accommodate this need in whatever ways it can, from worship times and styles to the different activities which it sponsors.

I saw a great example of this just a few weeks ago. I attended my first Gen X wedding in one of our local churches. The groom was a personal friend of my youngest son and the bride was the sister of one of my former students. As my wife and I arrived at the church we were greeted in the foyer by the members of the wedding party. The groom wore a bright red brocade jacket, black slacks, black and white saddle shoes and had dyed his hair orange/red to match his jacket. (The minister told me after the service that his hair was blue for the rehearsal!) The bride wore a long black dress with a white veil.

We were seated by a young usher, a high school friend of the groom. We had indicated that we were friends of the groom and had expected to be seated on the right side of the church, traditionally reserved for the groom's side. The usher took us down the aisle of the church, looked around, and seated us on the left. I turned to my wife with a puzzled look on my face and said, "Didn't we say 'Friends of the groom?'" She verified that indeed we had, but there was much more seating available on the bride's side. The Generation X usher was more highly motivated by what "worked" when it came to seating guests than "tradition." I thought it was fascinating that several other couples who had been seated on the bride's side, got up and moved over to the groom's side, even though there wasn't as much room there. (A testimony to a previous generation's need to do what is "right" and conventional.)

Before the ceremony started the parents were seated. The groom's parents had divorced and remarried when he was young, so his mother, stepfather, father and stepmother were all seated together in the same pew. Both the bride and the groom had a male and female attendant on each of their sides. This is very typical Xer as they are much less concerned about sexual differences and tradition. It really was quite a nice statement. It communicated the idea that friends from both sexes had played an important part in their growing up.

During the ceremony there were rings in abundance. Both the bride and groom exchanged rings as a part of their vows, they both wore a number of earrings, and there were even lip-ring studs on some of the Gen X guests. The attire of the guests was definitely Generation X. There was an abundance of black, brightly colored hair and one young man wore an old suit jacket with a T-shirt, tie around his neck, shorts and tennis shoes.

While the attire of most of the young guests and the atmosphere surrounding the wedding was very non-traditional, the important elements were still present. The deep love and commitment of the groom was evident as he shed tears of happiness as his bride came up the aisle to meet him. With great tenderness they exchanged their vows, pledging to love one another until death should separate them.

The reception was held in the new bride and groom's home instead of the fellowship hall of the church. While the entire ceremony was not carried out according to tradition, it was still very beautiful and the willingness of the church to accommodate the desires of this young couple without making a big deal out of it, went a long way to communicate the acceptance of them and honored their culture, friends and experiences.

Narrative Evangelism — The Powerful Use of Story

The postmodern mind has an aversion to any straightforward presentation of propositional truth as such, because it has abandoned its belief in absolute truth. The postmodern mind begins with the assumption that everything is relative, there is no absolute truth. It is highly skeptical of anyone or any institution claiming to possess absolute truth. How does the church, especially the preacher, break through that resistance to the concept of absolute truth and present the gospel message? The answer is the use of "story."

> The power of story is the power to infuse the mind with imagery so that it can vicariously undergo the events, experiences and feelings that take place in the story. According to Leighton Ford, story leads to a vision, and that vision produces a character. It doesn't just change a person's mind, as propositional arguments are intended to. It changes a person's outlook, worldview and paradigm.
>
> Story reaches not just the intellect. . . . Story reaches to the most deeply buried parts of the human personality, to the emotions, and even to that mysterious, elusive part of us that we know only as the human soul. A powerful story tingles our spine, surprises us with laughter, melts us to tears, moves us to righteous anger, tugs at our heartstrings, rivets our *psyche*, involves our *pneuma*, refashions our worldview, colors and filters our perspective, renegotiates our belief structure, calls into question our assumptions and ultimately leaves us a changed human being.[13]

Postmodernists are open to story. They believe that the sharing of one's story gives purpose and helps to shape social existence. They believe that all of life is a story and that every individual has a personal story. It is through the telling of one's story that an identity is formed.

> Story is a primary language of experience. Telling and listening to a story has the same structure as our experience. . . . The episodes of our lives take place one after another just like a story. One of the ways we know each other is by telling our stories. We live in stories.[14]

Eight Characteristics or Qualities of a Good Story

1. It has a single, clearly defined theme.
2. There is a single perspective from which the story develops.
3. It has a well-formed plot which moves from calm to conflict to resolution.
4. It makes use of realistic, graphic detail.
5. It makes an appeal to the senses whenever possible.
6. It only has a few major characters; lesser characters described only as necessary to the action.
7. There is a reliance on direct speech; feelings and motives mentioned only when essential for the point.
8. There is a judicious use of repetition, with end stress; that is, the most important thing is described last.

Source: Salmon, *Storytelling in Preaching*

Stories are a vehicle that the preacher can use to contemporize the gospel message. They will be readily received, understood and accepted.

To speak of contemporizing then, is to speak of restorying the gospel. Propositional statements may be necessary for theology, for exegesis, but they are not adequate for preaching. To say, "You are forgiven," or "God loves you," apart from the biblical story is almost meaningless. Similarly, to simply repeat the biblical story without making contact with our stories is not enough. But to connect the biblical events with the nitty-gritty happenings of our lives, ah, that is occasion for grace![15]

A good story conveys truth to the listener because it provides the listener with a picture of reality. Stories are attractive because they somehow shed light on the listener's own life. They allow people the chance to reflect upon their own life experience and find answers to their own problems. A preacher can incorporate the use of story deductively as an example to support the general proposition or particular truth that he is trying to convey, or he may use it inductively as an illustration to point analogically to a truth. Bruce Salmon points out, "Stories may be able to teach, console, and persuade more effectively than any other form of communication. Stories can focus experience even more forcefully than actual events."[16]

One must not confuse the use of story with fairy tales. Fairy tales are myths, made-up adventures about fictional characters in imaginary places performing unrealistic feats of strength or wisdom. Story is simple narrative, the retelling of one's encounters with all of life's problems, events and people. "Storytelling is profoundly biblical. There is an amazing amount of narrative material within Holy Scriptures."[17] As one reads through the Bible, a narrative thread which runs throughout is discovered. It is the story of redemption — God's plan to redeem fallen man. Most Christians were introduced to the Bible through its stories. Even before we had a grasp on the story's underlying theme, our imaginations were captured as we heard the stories about the adventures of God's people and his dealings with them.

The importance of the biblical story is seen in the fact that even before it was written down on parchment or tablets, it was passed down orally from generation to generation. Not only are these stories remembered, but they carry with them a force beyond that of the simple declarative statements which make up the essence of the story. As we read these stories, we identify with the characters, feel their anxiety and concerns and are caught up in the action of the plot. "Eventually, in some way the biblical story becomes our story. In the process, Scripture becomes forever contemporary, so that even in the midst of different historical circumstances, the story speaks forcefully to each new age."[18]

The value of a well-told story is that its action and characters resonate with something in the listener's own experience. This, in turn, causes the listener to identify with the main character in the story and to be open to truth or lesson which lies within.

Jesus recognized the importance of story and used it in his own preaching and teaching. Examine the Sermon on the Mount or the parables. Parables are simply short stories which have a hidden and deeper meaning behind them.

> Jesus understood the power of personal story when he interacted with the woman at the well. He knew her story and used its primary facts and symbols to win her. . . . The reason he was able to quickly build a rapport and win the hearing and faith of

200

this stranger was his knowledge and use of her personal story. A less effective approach would have started and finished with Jesus' own story of who he was. Of course, he did tell his own story, but when he did, it was woven in with hers.[19]

Storytelling is an especially effective tool with Generation X because it also facilitates a sense of community. "Persons who tell each other stories become friends. And men and women who know the same stories deeply are bound together in special ways."[20]

As our culture increasingly moves away from logic- and proposition-oriented thought forms and deeper into feelings-oriented and trans-rationally oriented thought forms, the only evangelism that speaks the language of the culture is a story-oriented evangelism. Narrative evangelism speaks the language of a media-saturated, story-hungry generation. It gives people a point of connection in their everyday lives, enabling them to see how God has interacted with human history and how he can interact with their own individual lives.[21]

Stories are powerful vehicles which enable us to make a connection with our target audience (Generation X), perhaps in a way that nothing else can. But there is an inherent danger in the use of narrative than one must be aware of, and that is the postmodern assumption that feelings and experience supersede logic and reason. The postmodernist would argue that subjective interpretation and application takes precedent over objective truth and evidence. It must be understood that a story is a good starting point, but it is not an end in and of itself. Jesus used stories in a powerful way for illustration and persuasion, but he never stopped with just the story. He always went on to appeal to the intellect and the will. A story can cause you to think. It can also cause you to feel. But that is not enough. Jesus always went on to call people to respond, to act and to commit themselves to the ramifications of their new insight gained from the story they had just heard.

Like Jesus, we have to go beyond stories. We have to state our truth. Stories can carry an enormous cargo of truth and meaning, but stories can't carry it all. If we do not make some propositional statements along with our storytelling, we fall into the trap of postmodernism, which suggests that all meaning resides in the hearer's interpretation of the story. As Christians we take the position that there truly is objective truth, and we will not allow our stories — or our Story with a capital S — to be left only to the subjective interpretation of the hearer.[22]

Process Evangelism

"What do Cinderella, princesses kissing frogs, and ugly ducklings have in common? All three describe a pilgrimage to beauty."[23] That sums up very well how effective evangelism with Generation X takes place — it is a process. Very rarely will an Xer have a Damascus road experience and fully commit himself to the Lord in light of one special event or encounter. For them, conversion is more of a slow, gradual process.

> The average nonbeliever is functionally insulated from the most common evangelistic approaches. . . . they do not attend revivals. They are not appreciative of door-to-door visits. They do not see a "Jesus Loves You" bumper sticker and feel like pulling off to the side of the road and repenting.[24]

The way the Generation X will be reached is when Christians intentionally build relationships with them and eventually share a verbal witness with them which is backed up by a credible lifestyle. This is the most effective form of evangelism with Generation X, and any others for that matter, who have grown up outside of the church and who are trying to make it in a postmodern world. It is simple — but effective.

The only problem is not with the strategy — it is with the insulated life of the average Christian. Most Christians do not have active, healthy relationships with non-Christians. All of their friends, and most of the events in their lives, are centered around the church or their family. Christians have withdrawn into holy huddles and Christian cliques. Sometimes, because of the political and social values that we derive from our commitment to Scripture, non-Christians are even viewed as the enemy!

But they are not the enemy — they are victims of the enemy. It still remains that the most effective means of evangelism with Generation X, or any other unbeliever, is within the context of a personal relationship where the right to be heard has been won. Nothing is more powerful than a personal testimony where the visible difference of the presence of Christ can be seen.

When dealing with Generation X, the Christian must commit himself to accepting the fact that conversion is going to take place over a longer period of time than it traditionally has in the past. The old techniques of street witnessing, sharing a tract with a stranger or cold-turkey calling are just not effective with this generation. In fact, they see the old *Evangelism Explosion* or *Four Spiritual Laws* presentation as a form of spiritual manipulation — guerrilla warfare tactics. (Sneak up on a person and hit them with the gospel before they know what is happening!) In process evangelism, people are convinced of the reality of God's love and the Christian message not by propositional arguments or one-time evangelistic rallies, but by a daily, consistent practical demonstration that Christianity works and that God's love is real. The key to the heart of Generation X is personal evangelism practiced by ordinary people with a heart and vision for taking the story of Jesus Christ to this generation, by going out into the world and purposely developing relationships with those who are lost.

There really are no "trade secrets" or special things that one needs to know in order to be successful at witnessing to Xers. It is all just common sense and the natural result of having developed a relationship with them. A good place to start if you have a desire to witness to Generation X is simply to do what they like to do. Buy some equipment and get involved in a street hockey team or go roller blading or snow boarding. Xers love physical activity, especially the ones that push them to the edge like rock climbing, rappelling, or bungee jumping.

Don't despair if you don't want to risk breaking your own neck in order to make some meaningful contacts. There are other ways to get to know members of Generation X. Hang out at your local coffee shop or go to a concert. Get involved in some local causes such as environmental concerns, feeding the homeless or political issues.

When you establish a contact, you must genuinely care about him or her. Xers can sniff out insincerity a mile away. If you are merely going through the motions you may turn him off to the gospel forever. He may already feel exploited and abused by the generation preceding him. If he picks up any indication that you have some ulterior motive behind your friendship, he will drop you like a hot potato. Evangelism with Generation X must never be a matter of simply "going through the motions." You must truly enjoy spending time with and talking to the people you are witnessing to, and enjoying the things you are doing with them. Anything less would be deceitful.

After you have established a secure relationship, you need to share Christ with them in terms they can understand. Be sure and de-church your vocabulary. Keep it matter-of-fact and straight up. Do emphasize the practical benefits of following Christ. Avoid any emotional manipulation or tear-jerking pleas. Don't use the hard-sell approach of a used-car salesman, but let it flow out naturally as you share your story and how it intersects with the story of Christ.

> Process evangelism that proceeds naturally out of real relationships breaks down the walls of distrust and wariness so that our story — our truth — can get through. Through the process of relationship building, pre-Christians can see the reality of our faith as we struggle to apply that faith to the problems and trials of our lives. The visible, tangible evidence of a Christian life being lived out under the pressures and stresses of a user-unfriendly world is the most convincing evidence we can possibly present in support of our story.[25]

The Need For a New Apologetic

Because of their postmodern worldview, which believes that there is no absolute truth, all things are relative, and which elevates feelings and experience to a level on par with, or even superior to, rational thought, Xers are not very responsive to traditional apologetic arguments for presenting the truth claims of the gospel. The postmodern worldview has feelings and intuition at its center, not rational thought and intellect. Xers are not as concerned with what one thinks, as much are they are with how something makes them feel.

Traditional apologetics has been built around the "evidences," logical reasons why the truth claims of the Bible are valid in light of the "facts" surrounding the construction of the Bible, the testimony of its witnesses, archaeological discovery, fulfilled prophecy and the superiority of its teachings. The typical way in which they would be used is that the Christian would build a case for the validity of the claims of Christianity much like a lawyer would, by piling up the evidence, one argument at a time. The idea behind it, is that all that the non-Christian needs in order to become a believer is to have all of his intellectual doubts and questions answered in a logical, rational way. Once all of his objections are refuted in light of the preponderance of the "evidence" on the side of the claims of Christianity, he is expected to make a decision for Christ.

But, for postmodernists, this evidential approach just doesn't cut it. After compiling all of your evidence and laying out your arguments for the validity of the Christian truth claims, you are just as likely to have an Xer respond with an apathetic "Whatever. . ." It is not that they don't understand your presentation, it is just that for them it is only one more point of view. You have your point of view, the Buddhists have theirs, and the New Agers have theirs. Since there are no absolute truths in their frame of reference, all of these religions and their accompanying truth claims are on equal footing.

So, how does one reach Generation X then? It's not going

to be by arguing with them, but it is by demonstrating authentic love and concern to them. When you reach out to them, stand by them through their struggles and problems, and open up your own life to them, the authenticity and transparency of your own Christian walk becomes the most persuasive presentation. Generation X hungers for friends who will be loyal and for relationships that will be genuine. They are seeking for a community of acceptance and affirmation. When they experience the same in the context of the church body, they will be open to accepting the beliefs of the Christians who have lived them out before them.

> . . . my generation demands a different apologetic — an embodied apologetic, a flesh-and-blood, living and breathing argument for God. The old apologetics of previous generations assumed that the barrier to conversion was intellectual and the way to remove that barrier was to answer all cognitive doubts. But Xers live in an age of intellectual ambiguity, when cognitive answers carry considerably less weight. The question my generation asks is not "Can Christians prove what they believe?" but "Can Christians live what they believe?"[26]

All of this is not to say that the intellectual dimension of faith is unimportant. There is still a place for using traditional apologetics — but it is with discipleship and not evangelism. After an Xer has been "loved into the kingdom" through the genuine and patient witness of a caring brother or sister, they need to grow in their understanding of the faith. So while apologetics may no longer be an effective witnessing tool, it can still be used as a very important anchor for securing the faith of new and growing Christians.

Ministry Through Small Groups

An effective way to attract Xers to a local congregation or campus fellowship is through the use of small groups. This is almost a necessity if a larger church hopes to draw members of Generation X into their fellowship. Through small groups you can provide a level of openness, relationship, sharing, empathy and healing that is not found in the larger context of the corporate body. Xers seek out community, closeness and fellowship. Small groups are the best way to meet that need.

While small groups have a lot of inherent potential for facilitating ministry, it must be stated up front that not all small groups are created equal. The combination of the personalities within the group, the stated purpose of the group and the quality of the group leadership all affect the dynamic of the group experience. Care must be taken in the selection of the group members, the training of the group leaders and the guidelines which will facilitate the group process.

There are a number of different types of small groups that a church may sponsor which members of Generation X might find appealing. The first is your basic support group. This is based upon the Alcoholics Anonymous model. The purpose of the group is to provide emotional support and helpful information for people who are struggling with a common problem such as alcohol and chemical addictions, physical and sexual abuse, eating disorders, dysfunctional families, divorce and grief issues.

The second type of group would be those which would come under the general heading of "didactic" which means teaching and learning. These could be Bible study groups, training groups for a specific ministry, leadership development or follow-up groups for new Christians to help ground them in the basic doctrines and beliefs of the church.

Why are small groups so appealing? What do people want from a small group experience? A number of things, actually. First of all, they simply want to be with their friends. A group experience is a great place just to hang together and learn more about one another's dreams, struggles and experiences. People want to talk. They want to express their feelings and ideas in a safe context and receive feedback from significant others about them. Xers especially want a place to belong. They have felt unwanted and rejected for so long, that it is refreshing to find a place where their presence is desired. Because many come from dysfunctional situations, they are also seeking to have some of their needs met by the group. People are also seeking answers. Growing Christians want instruction and greater insight. New believers want information and guidance in the Christian life. Lonely people are looking to build significant relationships.

What elements will affect the dynamic of each individual group? The basic relationships within the group have a great deal of influence upon the overall experience. If the leaders and group members already know one another, it is different than starting a group with a bunch of strangers. The different personality types within the group will also affect the group dynamic. It is important that the members are able to get along with one another and share a mutual respect for each other. The similarities and differences of group member's backgrounds will also have an effect on the group experience. Age differences, cultural differences, sex and educational backgrounds must all be taken into account when setting up the original group.

The leadership who are chosen to direct the group's activities will often determine the success or failure of the group. A desirable leader is one who has good interpersonal skills, adept at reading people's needs and responses. He or she must also be organized and disciplined. There is nothing more frustrating than going to a meeting with certain expectations and finding the leader inadequately prepared or late. Good communication skills are invaluable as a leader. A leader must be willing to spend time outside of the formal meetings with the individual members of the group.

The responsibilities of a group leader are many. His most obvious responsibility is to give direction to the group discussions and activities. He must keep the group on track. It is easy to get sidelined with peripheral issues or things that are not really conducive to spiritual growth or which fit in with the overall purpose and goals of the group. A good leader is able to ask stimulating questions and probes for answers. He provides a clear sense of purpose and vision for the group. He initiates activities for the group to participate in which serve to further solidify the sense of community and bonding between the individual members of the group. The leader is responsible for organizing the logistics of each meeting. He makes sure that the meeting time is the most convenient for the individual members and that the meeting room is reserved, chairs are set up, the temperature is comfortable and refreshments are available.

In order for a group experience to be positive, there need to be some "ground rules" which are accepted by all the members of the group and which direct the focus of the discussions. Three basic rules which I would suggest are:[27] 1) Be honest or be silent. Never force anyone to share. 2) Be totally confidential. Nothing which is shared in the group should be talked about outside of the confines of the group, especially if it is of a confidential nature. Trust is absolutely vital for the effective functioning of a small group. 3) Be committed to coming to the meeting. Healthy group dynamics depend upon a stable group. If different people show up every week, or if members only come hit-and-miss, the group will not function at its top potential.

It is important that members be accepting of one another, even if they disagree with another's thoughts or answers. Groups need to build one another up, and not tear down. Always try to affirm and encourage. Members must be respectful of one another. This means that individuals do not interrupt when another member of the group is talking. Group meetings are not places to make speeches or preach. They are to be avenues of mutual sharing and exchanging of ideas and insights. Last of all, the group should try to get every member involved in the discussion.

Small groups are needed because kids are LOST in the crowd, LONELY in an impersonal world, AFRAID to admit problems and reveal their true selves, and LEARNING to live. Having said all that, however, I must add a disclaimer — small groups per se will not guarantee successful ministry; they're not magic. Effective ministry is determined by a number of factors, including the needs and personalities of the kids, the environment, the skill of the minister, and, most important of all, the work of the Holy Spirit. But a small group can be an excellent way to provide the atmosphere for genuine ministry to occur.[28]

Reclaiming a Christian Worldview

Xers grew up in a postmodern, post-Christian culture. As such they espouse secular values and know very little about what God requires. They have no basis, other than themselves, for determining their ethics and values. The result is a society where human life is cheap and depravity reigns. Rape, murder, AIDS, crime, and immorality are the problems that we reaped when we abandoned our belief in God as a culture. It was not always this way. There was a time when society as a whole acknowledged God and His standards.

> While people have always committed sins, they at least acknowledged these were sins. A century ago a person may have committed adultery flagrantly and in defiance of God and man, but he would have admitted that what he was doing was a sin. What we have today is not only immoral behavior, but a loss of moral criteria. This is true even in the church. We face not only a moral collapse but a collapse of meaning. "There are no absolutes."[29]

Often people do not see the relationship between what they think and how they act. But the Bible says in Proverbs 23:7, "As a man thinketh in his heart, so is he." (KJV) Thinking affects behavior. A study was done by Josh McDowell to see what difference a belief in absolute truth made in the behavior of teenagers. He found that if a teenager did not accept an objective standard of truth, they became:

36% more likely to lie to you as a parent.
48% more likely to cheat on an exam.
2 times more likely to try to physically hurt someone.

2 times more likely to watch a pornographic film.
2 times more likely to get drunk.
2 and a quarter times more likely to steal.
3 times more likely to use illegal drugs.
6 times more likely to attempt suicide.[30]

How did we arrive at such a state? Everything has a starting point. For centuries in western culture, that starting point was the nature and character of God. All of life, all of existence, creation itself was grounded in the being of Jehovah God who was Lord over the universe. The meaning of human existence, truth and morality, was understood in the context of a universe inextricably linked to God's nature and character. A belief in the Triune God made sense of the whole of human experience and provided a valuable foundation for questions about right and wrong.

But in 1859 Charles Darwin published his *Origin of Species* and began to teach the theory of evolution. His theories were presented as a "scientific" alternative to the theistic understanding of origins. Evolutionary theory did away with the need for God — at least in the minds of those embracing this theory. Evolution put man at the center of his world and made him, not God, the arbiter of truth and morality.

This resulted in morality and truth being defined by the individual. It became a subjective and situational process. That means that every person decides for himself or herself whatever is right or wrong in any given circumstance — situation ethics. One might ask, "What is so wrong with this position? It seems fair, every person gets to decide for himself what is right for him without someone else imposing their values upon him. How can that be so bad?"

All one has to do is look at the history of Israel to learn this lesson. God first promised Abraham that he would make a great nation out of his descendants. After 450 years of captivity in Egypt, God led his people out of bondage with a mighty hand. He guided them to Mt. Sinai where he established his covenant with them and gave them his law — the Ten

211

Commandments. As long as the people were faithful to keep the law, an absolute standard, the nation prospered and every family was blessed. But after the conquering of the promised land under the leadership of Joshua, the generation who had seen the Lord's miracles died out. A new generation rose to power who did not honor the covenant or keep God's laws. They did "their own thing." The Bible says, "In those days Israel had no king; everyone did as he saw fit" (Judges 21:25).

What was the result of abandoning an absolute standard (the Law) and allowing individuals to determine what was right or wrong for themselves (situation ethics) in Israel? It meant 300 years of darkness and depravity. The period of the judges is one of the bleakest periods in the history of the nation of Israel. It is recorded during this period that men sacrificed their daughters, cut up their concubines, engaged in homosexuality and sexual immorality, rape, idolatry and deceit. But this should come as no surprise, because when you abandon a belief in an absolute moral standard, then no one can say with any authority that a particular act is right or wrong. Anything goes.

Listen to the words of Francis Schaeffer who said:

> If there is no absolute moral standard, then one cannot say in a final sense that anything is right or wrong. By absolute we mean that which always applies, that which provides a final or ultimate standard. There must be an absolute if there are to be morals, and there must be an absolute if there are to be real values. If there is no absolute beyond man's ideas, then there is no final appeal to judge between individuals and groups whose moral judgments conflict. We are merely left with conflicting opinions.[31]

Someone might admit, "Okay, I can see the need an absolute standard. But how can one determine what is right and what is wrong?" The best way to test any theory or truth claim, is to see how it works in the real world. Push it to the end of its logical conclusion and see if it will still hold up under the test of reality.

What we need is a two-step process that will, first test the truth to determine if it is absolute. This test compares a behavior or attitude to a standard of right and wrong that exists outside, above, and beyond ourselves. The next step. . . is to evaluate the evidence of truth to show how it actually works in reality. If a truth is right for all people, for all times, for all places, we should expect it to work adequately in the real world.[32]

Where does one come up with a standard that exists "outside, above, and beyond ourselves?" It is impossible to do so without bringing God into the equation. If an objective standard of right and wrong exists, it cannot be the product of the human mind because then it wouldn't be objective. It must be the product of another mind, a mind which is transcendent above human experience and knowledge. That mind is the mind of God. Absolute truth and morality reside with God, because they are a reflection of his character. Purity is right and immorality is wrong because God is a holy God. Fairness is right and cheating is wrong because God is a righteous God.

The reason the postmodern world cannot come up with an absolute standard of truth and morality is because their predecessors, the modernists, threw out all belief in God. Young people today cannot determine what is right and wrong because they do not know where all true values originate — with God. They must know God if they are to have an adequate base for determining right from wrong.

Once a belief in God is restored, then there can be a return to a Christian worldview. A Christian worldview provides meaning for existence and offers an absolute standard by which to judge all things. What a person believes really does make a difference in his or her ultimate behavior. This is never seen more clearly than when one compares the outcomes of competing worldviews.

A COMPARISON OF WORLDVIEWS						
	World	Time	Man	Ethics	Truth	Future
Judeo/ Christian	Created	Linear	Image of God	Absolutes/ God/Bible	Revelation/ Proposition	Resurrection/ Heaven or Hell
Humanism	Chance/ Evolution	Cyclical	Evolved Slime	Relative & Situational	Relative	Nihilism
New Age	Part of God	Cyclical	god	Relative & Internal	Channelers	Reincarnation

The Content of Our Programs

If the church hopes to attract members of Generation X to her activities and programs, there are certain elements which must be present. First of all, whatever you do must be done with quality and excellence. This is very important to Generation X. They have accepted the fact that they will be the first generation, as a whole, who will have lower incomes, fewer things and smaller homes than their parents. They are resigned to the fact that they will have less — but what they *do* have, they want to be quality. I can think of several examples where I have seen this played out.

Think of your typical neighborhood teenager. What kind of a car does he drive? Unless his parents are fairly well off and have provided it for him, it is probably going to be an older model that may have a few dents and dings with some rust spots and fading paint. It's not the Porsche of his dreams. However, *inside* that old bucket-of-bolts is a high dollar stereo! You can hear him coming five blocks away. Boom-boom-boom the music pounds out from the bass speakers. Your house shakes, your ears bleed and your animals run for cover. But he is making a statement for the whole world to hear. "I can't have it all — but what I do have is quality."

My youngest son, Caleb, got a job working at Famous Barr over the Christmas season. He was thrilled when he found out that as an employee he got a significant discount on his own purchases. He was bubbling with excitement as he told me about his latest purchase. "Dad, I got a pair of Silver Tabs,"

(Brand name blue jeans) "for only $45.00."

I was personally mortified that anyone would pay close to $50.00 for a pair of blue jeans, and especially shocked that he thought this was a bargain price. I pointed to the blue jeans that I was wearing at the time and said, "Caleb, Rustlers from Wal-Mart, only $9.95."

He was not impressed. His response was, "Yeah, Dad — Rustlers." His scorn was obvious. He would rather pay the high dollar for a fashion statement and a purchase of quality, than save money and wear an inexpensive pair of jeans. Remember, this is the generation that believes the commercial which says, "Image is everything."

Whatever your program, if it is going to connect with Generation X it must communicate quality. This is especially important in the promotional and recruitment material that goes out from the office. In this age of computers and laser printers, there is no excuse for a shabby looking, handwritten poster announcing some youth event. I can almost guarantee that any event that is advertised with a poor quality flyer will be avoided by the members of Generation X. Remember, to them "the medium is the message." If the advertisement is junk, they automatically assume that the event will be of poor quality also. The converse is also true. If the poster is cool, they will attend expecting the event to be dynamic as well.

Quality advertising is the first place you start. You won't even get invited into their lives without it. But you cannot stop there. Once you have tantalized them with great promotional materials, you must deliver what you have promised. They want a quality program. This means upbeat music, dynamic speakers, relevant topics, quick-paced action and an emphasis upon practical application.

The Christ In Youth Summer Conference programs are an excellent example of quality promotion and programming. The events are highly visual, action packed and a great effort is made to provide quality worship and speakers. The classes and activities offer a variety of practical choices and involve the students as much as possible. I have seen the Summer Conference program grow by the thousands and some church camp programs die a slow death. Why? One word — quality.

There also needs to be a variety of programs offered. While their parents grew up with only three basic TV channels to choose from, Xers are accustomed to cable. If they don't like what they see, they will switch in a minute. They are used to having many choices and a variety.

Xers are more likely to get involved on a personal level, rather than a group level. They want to know that an individual can make a difference in the world. They are looking for programs that will help them deal with some of their own personal problems, and avenues where their unique talents can be used to better the lives of others.

Let me give a word of caution here. It is impossible for one church to offer every program and meet every need that is crying out for attention in Generation X. Most churches just don't have that much volunteer help or the funding to support all of the programs needed.

But that is no reason for giving up in despair, either. The answer is "networking." If sister churches will work together for the common goal of reaching out to Generation X, then the needs will be met through cooperation. Each church needs to take inventory of the resources, both human and material, that is has to offer. Then, only do what you can do well. Offer programming in your area of strength and refer to other groups and other churches to meet needs that you are not prepared to handle. The spirit of cooperation will further promote a sense of community as the larger body of Christ works together for the greater good of the kingdom.

The programs, lessons, and preaching must also be practical and to the point. This is a generation that is ruled by pragmatism. Above all else, they want to know if it is going to work. "Show me that it works," said one man, "and then we can talk about whether or not it's true."[33] They are searching for real solutions to the pain and heartache that has characterized their lives. They don't care who won the battle of the Jebusites or how many angels can dance on the head of a pin. (Personally, I want to know what they are doing *dancing,* anyway!☺) Xers aren't concerned with theology or church polity. They want something that works. Issues that are of great importance to them and which they claim that the church has previously done a poor job are: avoiding substance abuse; developing leadership skills, developing meaningful relationships with other people; knowing how to communicate better with family; and doing better in school.[34]

What is done must be done with authenticity. Do everything with sincerity. Xers can spot a marketing gimmick light-years away. They don't want a "dog and pony" show. They want unity, love and acceptance. They want more than just fancy packaging; there must be substance. Xers prefer honesty over politeness. Don't worry so much about ceremony and manners — just give them the bottom line.

Go out of your way to let them know that they are genuinely wanted by God and by you for who they are right now (Psa. 68:5-6). Do whatever you can to help heal the rejection they may have felt from their own families and society by your acceptance and involvement in their lives. Provide them with models of healthy families and invite them to participate in your family activities. Honor their emphasis upon relationships over materialism. Teach them where true treasure is found (Matt. 6:19-24). Restore their sense of hope (Psa. 25:3; 33:13-20; 42:5; Rom. 8:18-25). Teach them that actions have consequences. Ethics must be based upon absolutes and cannot be situational (Gal. 6:7-10).

Teaching Generation X

My good friend Mark Moore, professor at Ozark Christian College, shared with me a handout that he prepared for one of his C.E. classes entitled "Teaching Generation X." While they were prepared with the college setting in mind, I believe that they will translate very nicely into the local church. Keep in mind that these guidelines apply to members of Generation X who have already made a commitment to Christ. Some of them may need to be modified if your audience makeup is basically non-Christian or pre-Christian. With his permission, I would like to pass on to you his excellent and very practical insights.

When teaching Generation X, understand that from their perspective nothing is sacred. They thrive on cynicism and will apply it liberally to "the sacred." They have been disillusioned by authority figures from Nixon to parents. Church leaders and teachers, therefore, must earn credibility the hard way. Until then, Xers will view them as fair game for demolition. In light of this, be genuine. Generation X can strip masks off in a hurry. Don't defend the indefensible. But also don't allow what is sacred to you to be scoffed. Wear thick skin. You are a target in their eyes the minute you step in front of a class or an audience. You can't avoid their cynicism, but you can outlive it. Provide "expedition" learning experiences which allow students to implement the theories of the classroom.

Xers need high touch. This is a love-starved generation. Most of their relationships have been dysfunctional. They have a general lack of respect for others as well as for themselves. Therefore, hug, touch and play . . . WITH CAUTION! Treat your students with respect. Treat them as people, not subjects or objects.

Generation X is notorious for their short attention spans. They love high-speed visual stimulus as well as trivia. Interest comes in short spurts but is not long-lived. They communicate in sound bites and slogans from movies and music. Therefore, the teacher who wants to communicate with Xers will need to master attention-getting techniques: movement, voice, visuals, alternative teaching methodologies. Break the curriculum down into smaller units. Remember, your job is not to entertain, but to educate; yet education will not take place when you have no one's attention. Listen to students' speech. Try to pick up on slogans, songs and movie lines. Those can be powerful attention grabbers.

They are bored. Humor is a badge of honor, especially nasty cynicism. In light of this it would be good to use humor liberally, but wisely. Be careful about your selection of jokes. Remember, whatever "lines" you bump up against, students will cross. This is especially true in what constitutes appropriate and inappropriate humor. Don't feed cynicism; it grows exponentially in students.

Xers are basically unshockable because they have been inundated with degenerate media. Their minds are filled with sexual images and language as well as violence and anger. In order to provide a more healthy and holy environment studiously avoid all references to sex unless absolutely necessary and only deal with it seriously. Raise and exemplify a higher ethical standard for students in your consumption of media and entertainment.

They are products of relativism. They have never been taught right from wrong, appropriate from inappropriate. They are confused about where to draw the line. As a result, they appreciate confrontational rebuke. Draw clear lines. Rebuke, exhort and chastise in love and privacy.

Generation X is very self-centered. When they talk out loud in class while the teacher is trying to lecture, they don't even think about the fact that it is rude — they can't imagine that a world exists outside of their own aura. For the good of the whole class and for the individual don't allow students to dominate, disrupt, sleep, or talk in class. Remind them consistently that they are a small part of a larger group. When you need to chastise students for doing these things, clearly articulate how you take their behavior personally. That is, tell them that what they do affects you and others.

They are experience oriented. They prefer to listen to stories rather than logic. They may not be religious, but they are quite spiritual, almost mystic. In order to take advantage of this tell stories, especially if you sense their attention waning. You probably don't need to defend the supernatural or the experiential. It will likely take longer for your students to really trust what you are saying and become convinced.

Conclusion

Generation X is seeking a challenge and a calling. They desperately desire some real heroes to follow and to pattern their lives after. They long for something in which to believe and commit themselves. Tony Campolo has written:

> I agree with (Ernest) Becker when he tells us that "youth was made for heroism and not for pleasure. . . ." We must inspire young people to greatness. By helping young people see themselves as agents of God's revolution, commissioned to a vocation of ultimate importance, we can provide them with a sense of calling that generates unparalleled enthusiasm for life. . . . We in youth work have mistakenly assumed that the best way to relate to young people is to provide them with various forms of entertainment. . . . Maybe we should instead invite our young people to accept the challenge to become heroes and change the world.[35]

Life Application and Implication For Ministry

1. Xers have grown up with a great deal of rejection. On a scale of 1-10, with a rating of 1 being very unwanted and a 10 being very wanted, how would you rate your church's or youth group's attitude toward members of Generation X? Especially those who dress in bizarre fashion and sport weird hair styles with bright colors? _____ What can be done to improve this?

2. Is your worship service "user-friendly" for an Xer? Do you:
   Explain what is going on during the service?
   Dechurch your vocabulary so that the man off the street would understand?
   Is there someone to greet them and direct them to an appropriate group as soon as they enter through the church doors?
   Is casual dress acceptable or is the rule "coat and tie?"
   Is the music a mixture of traditional and contemporary?

Do you make good and ample use of drama and multimedia in the service?

Do you provide excellent child-care facilities which are adequately sized, clean and well staffed?

Are the sermons focused on a practical application of the Christian life?

3. Do the teachers and preachers make good use of "story" as a communication device? Is there a place in your service or programming for others to tell their "story?"

4. Do the members of your church or youth group understand the basic principles behind process evangelism? What things are they doing which encourage the building of relationships with non-Christian members of Generation X?

5. Xers are much more experiential than cognitive. What events does your church sponsor which offer an entry-level experience for Xers into the basics of the Christian faith? What would it take to establish one?

6. What different small groups are available for Xers to become a part of? Does your church offer any leadership training for those responsible for a small group? What support groups are a part of the outreach ministry of your church? Singles? Divorce recovery? Alcoholics Anonymous? Sexual abuse? Eating disorders? Grief recovery?

7. Do the members of your youth group make their decisions based on absolutes or situation ethics? Do they know *why* some things are inherently right and some things are inherently wrong? Help them to be able to articulate all of the different aspects and ramifications of a Christian worldview and the difference it would make in their everyday lives.

8. Does the content of your church and youth group programs offer:

   Quality programming? Variety? Practical application? Networked to other churches? Authenticity?

9. Do you understand the basic principles of teaching Generation X? Can you handle cynicism? Do you use high touch with caution? Do you use humor? Do you make them

accountable and respectful to you as a teacher or leader? Do you try to incorporate creative teaching techniques, especially ones that strive for class participation and involvement?

Notes

1. Kevin Graham Ford, *Jesus For A New Generation*, 173.

2. Fran Sciacca, *Generation At Risk*, 27.

3. Gene Edward Veith, Jr., *Postmodern Times: A Christian Guide to Contemporary Thought and Culture* (Wheaton, IL: Crossway Books, 1994), 225.

4. Tim Smith, *Youthworker*, quoted in Mark DeVries, *Family-Based Youth Ministry: Reaching the Been-There, Done-That Generation* (Downers Grove, IL: InterVarsity Press, 1994), 58.

5. George Barna, *Generation Next*, 59.

6. Romans 5:10-11; 11:15; 2 Corinthians 5:18-20; Colossians 1:19-22.

7. Isaiah 53:3.

8. James Emery White, "Evangelism in a Postmodern World," in *The Challenge of Postmodernism: An Evangelical Engagement*, ed. David S. Dockery (Wheaton, IL: A BridgePoint Book, 1995), 367.

9. Gary L. McIntosh, *Three Generations: Riding the Waves of Change in Your Church* (Grand Rapids: Fleming H. Revell, 1995), 157.

10. Ibid., 158.

11. White, "Evangelism," 366.

12. Ibid., 367.

13. Ford, *Jesus For A New Generation*, 225.

14. Thomas E. Boomershine, *Story Journey: An Invitation to the Gospel as Storytelling* (Nashville: Abingdon Press, 1988),18.

15. Bruce Salmon, *Storytelling in Preaching: A Guide to the Theory and Practice* (Nashville: Broadman Press, 1988), 33.

16. Ibid., 39.

17. Ibid., 25.

18. Ibid., 26.

19. Leith Anderson, *A Church For the 21st Century: Bringing Change to Your Church to Meet the Challenges of a Changing Society* (Minneapolis: Bethany House, 1992), 113.

20. Boomershine, *Story Journey*, 18.

21. Ford, *Jesus For A New Generation*, 221.

22. Ibid., 236.

23. Joseph C. Aldrich, *Life-Style Evangelism: Crossing Traditional Boundaries to Reach the Unbelieving World* (Portland, OR: Multnomah Press, 1981), 25.

24. White, "Evangelism," 367.

25. Ford, *Jesus For A New Generation*, 199.

26. Ibid., 174.

27. Dave Bartlett, *Honest to God* (Youth for Christ/USA, 1989), 3-4.

28. David, R. Veerman, *Small Group Ministry With Youth* (Wheaton, IL: Victor Books, 1992), 20.

29. Veith, *Postmodern Times*, 18.

30. Josh McDowell and Bob Hostetler, *Right From Wrong: What You Need to Know to Help Youth Make Right Choices* (Dallas: Word, 1994), 18.

31. Francis Schaeffer, *How Should We Then Live?* 145.

32. McDowell and Hostetler, *Right From Wrong*, 79.

33. White, "Evangelism," 370.

34. George Barna, *Baby Busters*, 142.

35. Anthony Campolo, *Growing Up In America: A Sociology of Youth Ministry* (Grand Rapids: Zondervan, 1989), 33, 153.

OUTLINE
THE NEXT GENERATION: UNDERSTANDING AND MEETING THE NEEDS OF GENERATION X

INTRO: Tim's story

PART I — THE CHARACTERISTICS OF GENERATION X

I. Who Is Generation X?
   A. Birth Year Boundaries
      1. Born from 1961-1981 (Howe & Strauss)
      2. Born from 1965-1983 (George Barna)
      3. Born from 1960-1980 (Geoffrey Holtz)
      4. Born from 1963-1984 (Kennedy Assassination)
   B. They Hate Labels
      1. Positive ones tried at first
      2. Negative labels seemed better suited to the times and situation
      3. Most common are:
         a. Baby Busters
         b. 13th Gen
         c. Generation X
      4. What's so important about a name?

II. The Most Unwanted Generation
   A. Birth Control Factor
   B. Abortion
   C. Zero Population Growth
   D. Latchkey Kids — 10 Million Under the Age of 14
   E. Working Mothers
   F. Day Care
   G. Housing Laws

        1. Not until 1988 did Congress amend the Civil Rights Act
        2. 70-90% in large cities were strictly adults only
    H. Movies, Restaurants, and the Swinging Singles
        1. Children in years preceding
        2. New Genre of "children are evil" movies
    I. Baby On Board

III. Dysfunctional Families
    A. Rising Divorce Rate
    B. Effect of Divorce on Kids
    C. Blended Families
    D. Single-Parent Families
    E. Dysfunctional Intact Families
    F. Physical and Sexual Abuse
    G. Drug and Alcohol Addictions

IV. The Education of Generation X
    A. Lowest SAT and ACT Scores in Years
    B. Scores Fell and Grades Rose
    C. Biblical Ignorance
    D The Why Behind the Fall
        1. Abandonment of absolutes
        2. "Open" classroom structure
        3. Self-esteem is major goal
    E Incompetent Teachers
    F. How It All Played Out For Generation X

V. The Values and Beliefs of Generation X
    A. Pragmatic - "Just Do It!"
    B. Involved On an Individual Level — Not the Group Level
    C. Exit Absolute Truth
    D. Smorgasbord Spirituality
    E. The Politics of Generation X
    F. The Sex Generation
    G. Concerns of Generation X Teens
        1. Education
        2. Relationships
        3. Emotional pressure
        4. Physical threats

    5. Financial concerns
  H. Post Traumatic Stress Disorder
  I. Generation X and the Workplace

VI. An Overview and Summary
  A. Schoolhouse Woes
  B. Soaring Crime
  C. Stress, Suicide and Mental Health
  D. Sexual Activity and Consequences
  E. Teenage Runaways and Throwaways
  F. Trauma and Survivor's Guilt
  G. Hostility
  H. Darkness on the Horizon
  I. Are There Any Exceptions?
  J. Differences Between Boomers and Generation X

PART II — UNDERSTANDING THE HISTORY OF GENERATION X

VII. Worldview
  A. The Theistic Worldview
  B. The Modern Worldview
  C. Summary
  D. A Comparison Between the Worldviews of Theism and Modernism

VIII. The Development of a Postmodern Worldview
  A. The Star Trek Analogy
  B. Deconstruction
  C. Everything is Relative
  D. What Are the Implications For the Church?

PART III — UNDERSTANDING AND MEETING THE NEEDS OF GENERATION X

IX. Comparing Two Worlds
  A. A Loss of Center
  B. Biblical Illiteracy
  C. Family Fragmentation
  D. Secularization of the People of God
  E. Legalism On Horizon to Protect Perimeters
  F. Religion of Form — Little Substance
  G. Neglect of Personal Holiness and Piety

      H. Stress Level High Over Lack of Control Over One's Destiny

      I. Conclusion

X. Gateways to the Soul of Generation X

    A. The Need For Community

    B. Spirituality

    C. Sexuality

    D. Mystery

    E. Relationships Versus Race and Possessions

    F. Family

    G. Identity

    H. Involvement In Causes

    I. Conclusion

XI. Programming to Meet the Needs of Generation X

    A. Creating a User-Friendly Environment

      1. Explain what and why you do things

      2. Dechurch your vocabulary

      3. Informal dress and setting

      4. Creativity and excitement

      5. Quick paced

      6. Recognition — but not spotlighted

      7. A good first impression

      8. Excellent child care facilities

      9. Practical messages

     10. Variety and diversity

    B. Narrative Evangelism — The Powerful Use of Story

      1. Characteristics or qualities of a good story

      2. The need to contemporize the gospel story

      3. Do not confuse story with fairy tales

      4. Story is an effective tool

    C. Process Evangelism

    D. The Need For a New Apologetic

    E. Ministry Through Small Groups

      1. Many different kinds of small groups

      2. The makeup of a small group

      3. The leadership of a small group

    F. Reclaiming a Christian Worldview

    G. The Content of Our Programs

1. Quality and excellence
2. A variety of choices
3. Networking
4. Practical and to the point
5. Authenticity

H. Teaching Generation X
I. Conclusion

BIBLIOGRAPHY

"Abortion In the Church." *Current Thoughts & Trends,* 11 January 1995, 30.

"Absentee Dads." *Current Thoughts & Trends,* 8 July 1992, 11.

"Adults-Only Housing Hears the Pitter Patter of Little Feet." *Business Week,* 13 March 1989.

Aldrich, Joseph C. *Life-Style Evangelism: Crossing Traditional Boundaries to Reach the Unbelieving World.* Portland, OR: Multnomah Press, 1981.

Allen, Diogenes. *Christian Belief In A Postmodern World.* Louisville: John Knox Press, 1989.

Allen, Gary. "The Grave National Decline in Education." *American Opinion,* 22 March 1979, 1-4.

"And Where's Dad?" *Current Thoughts & Trends,* 9 October 1993, 15.

Anderson, Leith. *A Church For the Twenty-first Century: Bringing Change to Your Church to Meet the Challenges of a Changing Society.* Minneapolis: Bethany House, 1992.

Armstrong, Darrell. "The Fire Within." *Sojourners,* November 1994, 18.

Barna, George. *Baby Busters: The Disillusioned Generation.* Chicago: Northfield Publishing, 1992.

————. *The Future of the American Family.* Chicago: Moody Press, 1993.

————. *Generation Next: What Every Parent and Youthworker*

Needs to Know About the Attitudes and Beliefs of Today's Youth. Glendale, CA: Barna Research Group, 1995.

—————. *Today's Teens: A Generation in Transition.* Glendale, CA: Barna Research Group, 199.

Barringer, Felicity. "Report Finds 1 in 5 Infected by Viruses Spread Sexually." *New York Times,* 1 April 1993, p. A1.

Bartlett, Dave. *Honest to God.* Youth for Christ/USA, 1989.

Barton, Charles. *The Myth of Separation.* Aledo, TX: Wall Builder Press, 1991.

Becker, Ernest. *The Denial of Death.* New York: The Free Press, 1973.

Bennett, William. "Boys to Men." *Current Thoughts & Trends,* 11 June 1995, 18.

—————. *The Index of Leading Cultural Indicators.* Empower America, The Heritage Foundation & Free Congress Foundation, Vol 1 (March 1993).

Benson, Warren S. and Senter, Mark H. III, eds. *The Complete Book of Youth Ministry.* Chicago: Moody Press, 1987.

Berkhof, L. *Systematic Theology.* Grand Rapids: Eerdmans, 1939.

Bezilla, Robert, ed. *America's Youth 1977-1988.* Princeton, NJ: The Gallup Organization, 1988.

—————, ed. *America's Youth in the 1990s.* Princeton, NJ: The George H. Gallup International Institute, 1993.

Bloom, Allan. *The Closing of the American Mind.* New York: Simon & Schuster, 1987.

Blumenfeld, Samuel L. *NEA: Trojan Horse in American Education.* Boise, ID: The Paradigm Co., 1984.

Boomershine, Thomas E. *Story Journey: An Invitation to the Gospel as Storytelling.* Nashville: Abingdon Press, 1988.

Boyer, Ernest L. *High School: A Report on Secondary Education in America.* New York: Harper & Row, 1983.

Brisco, Tommy. "Mystery Religions." Holman Bible Dictionary, Quick Verse. Hiawatha, IA: Parsons Technology.

Brown, Harold O. J. "Abortion Stats In Perspective." *Current Thoughts & Trends,* 11 June 1995, 20.

Campolo, Anthony. *Growing Up In America: A Sociology of Youth Ministry.* Grand Rapids: Zondervan, 1989.

Christensen, Bryce. "Cohabitation Fails Expectations." *The Joplin Globe,* 5 November 1989, p. 6A.

Colson, Chuck. *Kingdoms in Conflict.* Grand Rapids: Zondervan, 1989.

Coupland, Douglas. *Generation X: Tales For An Accelerated Culture.* New York: St. Martin's Press, 1991.

————. *Life After God.* New York: Pocket Books, 1994.

Darnton, Nina. "Committed Youth," *Newsweek,* 31 July 1989, 66-72.

Dausey, Gary. *The Youth Leader's Sourcebook.* Grand Rapids: Zondervan, 1983.

"Day Care Detriment." *Current Thoughts & Trends,* 11 November 1995, 12.

DeVries, Mark. *Family-Based Youth Ministry: Reaching the Been-There, Done-That Generation.* Downers Grove: Inter-Varsity, 1994.

Dobson, James C. and Bauer, Gary L. *Children At Risk: Winning the Battle for the Hearts and Minds of Your Children.* Dallas: Word Publishing, 1990.

Dockery, David S. ed. *The Challenge of Postmodernism: An Evangelical Engagement.* Wheaton, IL: Victor Books, 1995.

Dunn, William. *The Baby Bust: A Generation Comes of Age.* Ithaca, NY: American Demographics Books, 1993.

"Earnings on the Job." *The Youth Ministry Resource Book.* Loveland, CO: Group Books, 1988, 87.

"Educational Malaise." *Current Thoughts & Trends,* 9 February 1993, 25.

Ehrlich, Paul R. *The Population Bomb.* New York: Random House, 1968.

Einstein, Elizabeth. *The Stepfamily: Living, Loving & Learning.* Boston: Shambhala, 1985.

"Empty Houses, Empty Children." *Current Thoughts & Trends,* 10 August 1994, 13.

Encyclopaedia Judaica, 2nd ed., s.v. "Name, Change of."

Endsley, Malissa. "Understanding Generation X." *ACU Today,* Spring 1995, 12.

"Facts About Families." *Current Thoughts & Trends,* 9 August 1993, 14.

Famighetti, Robert, ed. *The World Almanac and Book of Facts.* Mahwah, NJ: St. Martin's Press, 1995.

Feder, Don. "Independence Day: A Nation in Historical Denial." *Orange County Register,* 4 July 1993.

Ford, Kevin Graham. *Jesus For A New Generation: Putting the Gospel in the Language of Xers.* Downers Grove: Inter-Varsity Press, 1995.

Frydenger, Tom & Adrienne. *The Blended Family.* New York: Chosen Books, 1984.

Goethe, Johann. "The Beginning (and the end) of Civilization." *Current Thoughts & Trends,* 11 February 1995, 18.

Goldman, Bob. *Death In The Locker Room.* South Bend, IN: Icarus, 1984.

Goleman, Daniel. "Teen-Agers Called Shrewd Judges of Risk." *New York Times,* 1 March 1993, p. B5.

Grenz, Stanley J. "Postmodernism and the Future of Evangelical Theology: *Star Trek* and the Next Generation." *Evangelical Review of Theology,* 18 October 1994, 324.

Gulley, Normal R. "Reader-Response Theories in Postmodern Hermeneutics: A Challenge to Evangelical Theology," in David S. Dockery, ed., *The Challenge of Postmodernism: An Evangelical Engagement.* Wheaton, IL: Victor Books, 1995, 220-221.

Hart, Archibald D. *Children & Divorce: What to Expect: How to Help.* Waco: Word, 1982.

Harvey, David. *The Condition of Postmodernity.* Cambridge, MA: Basil Blackwell, 1989.

"Health Report," *Time,* 30 August 1993, 16.

"Help, Teacher Can't Teach." *Time,* 16 June 1980, 55.

Holtz, Geoffrey T. *Welcome to the Jungle: The Why Behind "Generation X."* New York: St. Martin's Griffin, 1995.

Howe, Neil and Strauss, Bill. *13th Gen: Abort, Retry, Ignore,*

Fail? New York: Vintage Books, 1993.

Humanist Manifestos I and II. Buffalo: Prometheus Books, 1973.

Janssen, Al and Weeden, Larry K., eds. *Seven Promises of a Promise Keeper.* Colorado Springs: Focus on the Family Publishing, 1994.

Johnston, Jerry. *Why Suicide?* New York: Oliver Nelson, 1987.

Jones, Milton. "Bringing the Cross to Generation X." *Image,* July-August 1994, 23-26.

Kerbel, Jarrett. "Generation's Faith." *Sojourners,* November 1994, 15.

Klaus, Tom. *Healing Hidden Wounds: Ministering to Teenagers From Alcoholic Families.* Loveland, CO: Group Books, 1989.

Kotulak, Ronald. "Growing Up At Risk: Dangerous Passage." *Chicago Tribune,* 7 December 1986, Sec 6 p.1.

Ladd, Everett C. "Exposing the Myth of the Generation Gap." *Reader's Digest,* January 1995, 49-54.

LaHaye, Tim. *The Battle for the Public Schools: Humanism's Threat to our Children.* Old Tappan, NJ: Fleming H. Revell Company, 1983.

LaHaye, Tim & Beverly. *A Nation Without A Conscience.* Wheaton, IL: Tyndale House Publishers, 1994.

Laiken, Deidre S. *Daughters of Divorce: The Effects of Parental Divorce On Women's Lives.* New York: William Morrow, 1981.

Leary, Warren E. "Gloomy Report on the Health of Teenagers." *New York Times,* 9 June 1990, 24.

Leerhsen, Charles. "Alcohol and the Family." *Newsweek,* 18 January 1988, 63.

Lipsky, David and Abrams, Alexander, "The Packaging (and Re-Packaging) of a Generation." *Harpers Magazine,* July 1994, 20.

Louv, Richard. *Childhood's Future: Listening to the American Family. New Hope for the Next Generation.* Boston: Houghton Mifflin, 1990.

Lowell, Piper. "Out of Desperation." *Sojourners,* November 1994, 20.

235

————. "Generation's Faith." *Sojourners*, November 1994, 20.

Lytle, Vicky. "Children of Alcoholics: Recognizing Their 'Secret Suffering'. *NEA Today*, December 1987, 9.

Mahedy, William and Bernardi, Janet. *A Generation Alone: Xers Making a Place in the World*. Downers Grove: InterVarsity Press, 1994.

Martin, David. "The Whiny Generation." *Newsweek*, 1 November 1993, 10.

Mars Hill Productions, 12705 South Kirkwood STE. 218, Stafford, Texas 77477.

Marvel, Bill and Morrison, Melissa. "The Pacifier People." *The Dallas Morning News*, F4.

Mayfield, Mark. "Assaults Top the List of Classroom Chaos." *USA Today*, 8 December 1986, p. 10A.

McDowell, Josh. *How To Help Your Child Say "No" To Sexual Pressure*. Waco: Word Books, 1987.

McDowell, Josh and Day, Dick. *Why Wait?: What You Need to Know About the Teen Sexuality Crisis*. San Bernardino, CA: Here's Life Publishers, 1987.

McDowell, Josh and Wakefield, Norm. *The Dad Difference*. San Bernardino, CA: Here's Life, 1989.

McIntosh, Gary L. *Three Generations: Riding the Waves of Change in Your Church*. Grand Rapids: Fleming H. Revell, 1995.

McLeod, Mark S. "Making God Dance: Postmodern Theorizing and the Christian College." *Christian Scholar's Review*, 21 March 1992, 279.

McNeal, T. R. "Work, Theology of," Holman Bible Dictionary, Quick Verse, Hiawatha, IA: Parsons Technology.

Medawar, Peter. "On 'The Effecting of All Things Possible.'" *The Listener*, 2 October 1969, 7.

Miller, James B. "The Emerging Postmodern World." In *Postmodern Theology: Christian Faith in a Pluralist World*, ed. Frederic B. Burnham. New York: Harper & Row, 1989, 9.

Moore, David T. *Five Lies of the Century*. Wheaton, IL: Tyndale

House Publishers, 1995.

Nash, Ronald H. *The Closing of the American Heart: What's Really Wrong With America's Schools.* Probe Books, 1990.

The National Commission on Excellence in Education, *A Nation at Risk: The Full Account.* Cambridge, MA: U.S.A. Research, 1984.

Nelson, Rob & Cowan, Jon. *Revolution X: A Survival Guide For Our Generation.* New York: Penguin Books, 1994.

Nethaway, Rowland. "Missing Core Values." Cox News Service appearing in the *Hamilton (OH) Journal-News,* 3 November 1993.

Oden, Thomas. "Back to the Fathers." Interview by Christopher Hall, *Christianity Today,* 24 September 1990, 28-31.

————. *Two Worlds: Notes On the Death of Modernity in America & Russia.* Downers Grove, IL: InterVarsity Press, 1992.

Parker, Christina. *Children of Alcoholics: Growing Up Unheard.* Phoenix, AZ: Do It Now Foundation, 1986.

"Perils Cited for Latchkey Children." *Youthletter,* March 1986, 3.

Powell, John. *Abortion: The Silent Holocaust.* Allen, TX: Argus Communications, 1981.

Ravitch, Diane. *The Schools We Deserve.* New York: Basic Books, 1985.

Roehlkepartain, Eugene C. ed. *The Youth Ministry Resource Book.* Loveland, CO: Group Books, 1988.

Rushkoff, Douglas. *The Gen X Reader.* New York: Ballantine Books, 1994.

Salmon, Bruce. *Storytelling in Preaching: A Guide to the Theory and Practice.* Nashville: Broadman Press, 1988.

Schaeffer, Francis A. *How Should We Then Live?: The Rise and Decline of Western Thought and Culture.* Old Tappan, NJ, Fleming H. Revell, 1976.

Schneiders, Sandra M. "Does the Bible Have a Postmodern Message?" in *Postmodern Theology: Christian Faith in a Pluralist World.* ed. Frederic B. Burnham, New York:

Harper & Row, 1989, 61-62.

Sciacca, Fran. *Generation at Risk: What Legacy Are the Baby-Boomers Leaving Their Kids?* Chicago: Moody Press, 1990.

Scott, Otto. "Psychiatry Discovers Religion." *Chalcedon Report*, no. 345, April 1994, 3.

Simms, Margaret C. *Families and Housing Markets: Obstacles to Locating Suitable Housing.* HUD, 1980.

"Single Parents: Never-Marrieds Soon to Outnumber Divorced." *Current Thoughts & Trends*, 11 March 1995, 10.

Sire, James W. *The Universe Next Door: A Basic World View Catalog.* Downers Grove, IL: InterVarsity Press, 1976.

Sizemore, Finley H. *Suicide: The Signs and Solutions.* Wheaton, IL: Victor Books, 1988.

Smith, Franci and Coleman, Susan. "Battered Women." The New Grolier Electronic Encyclopedia, The Software Toolworks, Inc, 1993, paragraph 1.

Sommerville, John. *The Rise and Fall of Childhood.* New York: Vintage Books, 1982.

Sowell, Thomas. *Inside American Education*: The Decline, The Deception, The Dogmas. New York: The Free Press, 1993.

Spencer, Rich. "'Discarded' Child Population Put at Nearly 500,000." *Washington Post*, 12 December 1989, A1.

"Squeezing Into the '70s." *Life*, 9 January 1970, 8.

Star, Alexander. "The Twentysomething Myth." *The New Republic*, January 4 & 11, 1993, 22.

Strauss, William and Howe, Neil. *Generations: The History of America's Future, 1584 to 2069.* New York: Quill, 1991.

Strommen, Merton and Irene. *The Five Cries of Parents.* San Francisco: Harper, 1985.

Tapia, Andres. "Reaching the First Post-Christian Generation." *Christianity Today*, 12 September 1994, 21.

Thomas, Steve. *Your Church Can Be. . . Family Friendly: How You Can Launch a Successful Family Ministry in Your Congregation.* Joplin, MO: College Press, 1996.

"Throwaway Kids." *Newsweek*, 25 April 1988, 65.

Titus, Harold H. and Smith, Marilyn S. *Living Issues In Philosophy.* New York: D. Van Nostrand Company, 1974.

Van Gelder, Craig. "Postmodernism As An Emerging Worldview." *Calvin Theological Journal,* 26 1991, 412.

Veerman, David. R. *Small Group Ministry With Youth.* Wheaton, IL: Victor Books, 1992.

Veith, Gene Edward, Jr. *Postmodern Times: A Christian Guide to Contemporary Thought and Culture.* Wheaton, IL: Crossway Books, 1994.

Wallis, Claudia. "Children Having Children." *Time,* 9 December 1985, 78-90.

Walters, Barbara. "America's Kids, Why They Flunk," a television special.

Walters, Laura Sherman. *There's A New Family In My House!: Blending Stepfamilies Together.* Wheaton, IL: Harold Shaw Publishers, 1993.

Webster, Noah. *The History of the United States.* New Haven, CT: Durrie & Peck, 1832.

"What Is So Unique About Generation X?" *Current Thoughts & Trends,* 11 June 1995, 30.

White, James Emery. "Evangelism in a Postmodern World," in David S. Dockery, ed., *The Challenge of Postmodernism: An Evangelical Engagement.* Wheaton, IL: Victor Books, 1995, 362-363.

Whitehead, Barbara DaFoe. "Dan Quayle Was Right." *The Atlantic Monthly,* April 1993, 62.

The Zondervan Pictorial Encyclopedia of the Bible, 4th ed., s.v. "Name" and *The Interpreter's Dictionary of the Bible,* 1st ed., s.v. "Name."

INDEX

Abortion, 29, 31, 95

Abuse, 47, 50, 51-52, 53

ACT & SAT test scores, 59-60, 66, 86, 96

AIDS, 83-84

Anger, 22, 91, 165

Ann Landers survey, 30

Apologetics, 166, 205

Assassination of JFK, 20

Baby On Board, 37

Baby Busters, 19-20, 21

Barna, George, 19, 21, 78, 79

Biblical illiteracy, 62-63, 156-157

Birth control, 20, 29-30, 95

Birth years of Generation X, 19-20

Blended famlies, 46-48

Boomers, 21, 37, 66, 75, 83, 86, 113, 179-180

Builders, 21, 83

Causes, involvement in, 72-73, 182

Center, a loss of, 152-156

Childless to child-free, 30

Children of alcoholics, 52-54

Clay jar, treasures in, 24

Community, 167-171

Cohabitation, 175-176

Concerns of Generation X, 86-88

Crime, 44, 96-97

Cynicism, 20, 103, 218

Daycare, 34

Deconstruction, 136-140

Differences between Boomers & Xers, 113

Divorce, 14, 42-44, 95, 175, 181

effects of divorce, 44-46

Drug and alcohol addiction, 52-54

Economic issues, 44, 80

Education, 45, 86

Equal Access Act, 173

Evolution, 211

Family, definition of, 168-169, 181

family fragmentation, 157

stress on family, 182

Feelings, 76

Friends, 87, 167-168

Gallup Survey, 60

Gangs, 84

Gay rights, 81

Generation X, 20, 21

God, belief in, 77-79

Grades, 61

Hostility, 102-103

Housing laws, 35-36

Identity, 184-185

Illiteracy, 59-62

Image of God, 116-118, 119

Incest, 51-52

Intact families, 49-51

"Just Do It," 72

Labels, 21-24

Latchkey kids, 32-33

Legalism, 158-160

Materialism, 179-180

Moral Standards, 99, 142, 154-156, 210-213

Motherhood, 41-42

Movies, 36

Mystery, 176-177

Names, for Generation X, 21-22, 24
  importance of, 24
  and O.T., 25
  and Talmud, 25
Narrative evangelism, 197-202
National debt, 80
Open education, 66-67
Parenting, 37
Peer pressure, 50
Pessimism, 43
Politics, 79-82
Postmodernism, 113, 131-136, 142-146
Process evangelism, 202-204
Programming for Generation X, 214-217
Race, 177-178
Relationships, importance of, 177-178
Relativism, 64-65, 140-143
Rogers, Carl, 66-67
Runaways, 51, 100
Secularization and the people of God, 157-158
See You At The Pole, 173
Self-esteem, 61, 67-69
Sexual abuse, 47, 51-52, 95
Sexual attitudes of Generation X, 82-85, 98-100, 174-176
Sexual tempation, 50
Short-term missions, 174
Single parents, 48-49
Small group ministry, 206-210
  support groups, 207
  leadership training, 208-209
Social Security, 80, 91
Spirituality, 78-79, 104-105, 171-174

Star Trek, 134-136
STD'S, 84-85, 99
Story, 197-202
Stress, 87, 97, 161-162
Suicide, 97-98
Survivor's guilt, 100-102
Teachers, 65, 66
Teaching Generation X, 217-219
Teenage pregnancy, 99
Theodore Roosevelt, 41, 42
Thirteenth Generation, 22
Time spent with family, 34, 47-48, 49-51
Tolerance, 64
Treasure, 24
True Love Waits, 173-174
Truth, 64
  belief in absolute truth, 76, 210-213
Unwanted, 37-38, 95
User-friendly churches, 192-197
Values, 64
Work, attitudes of Xers, 88-89
  effects of after school jobs, 90
  minimum wage, 91
Worldview, 113, 213-214
  Deism, 121-123, 126-127
  Theistic worldview, 115, 120-121, 126, 210-211
  Modern worldview, 121, 127, 132, 141, 144
  Naturalism, 123-125
Working mothers, 32-35
Worship services for Generation X, 192-196
Xer, 23
Zero population growth, 31-32

About the Author

Gary Zustiak is Professor of Youth Ministry and Psychology at Ozark Christian College. He has served as Associate Minister in Sandpoint, Idaho, Preaching Minister in Broadwell, Illinois, and Youth Minister in Farmer City, Illinois and in Emmett, Idaho. Gary has also served as Chaplain for Deaconess Hospital in Spokane, Washington and Logan Correctional Center in Lincoln, Illinois. Dr. Zustiak received the B.A. from Boise Bible College, M.A. in Pastoral Care and Counseling and M.Div. in Christian Ministry from Lincoln Christian Seminary, and D.Min. in Marriage and Family from Abilene Christian University.

Gary has written articles for *The Christian Standard*, *The Lookout*, and contributed regularly to *Youth Worker Update*. He is listed in *Who's Who in America*, *Outstanding Young Men of America*, and *Who's Who in the Midwest*. His wife, Mary, is a graduate of Missouri Southern State College and currently serves as a registered nurse for St. John's Hospital. They have three sons: Joshua, in the Air Force; Aaron, a student at Ozark Christian College; and Caleb, a student at Southeast Missouri State University. Gary enjoys Tae Kwon Do, chess, music and playing with his granddaughter, Alicia Kye, as well as coaching soccer at Ozark.